Elsie Roxborough with sister Vergie and friends from the University of Michigan pose on the beach in front of the Idlewild Clubhouse and Idlewild Lake. (From the private collection of Carol Roxborough-Nakanishi.)

IMAGES
of America

IDLEWILD

THE BLACK EDEN OF MICHIGAN

IMAGES
of America

IDLEWILD

THE BLACK EDEN OF MICHIGAN

Ronald J. Stephens

ARCADIA
PUBLISHING

Published by Arcadia Publishing
Charleston, South Carolina

Library of Congress Catalog Card Number: 2001091396

For all general information contact Arcadia Publishing at:
Telephone 843-853-2070
Fax 843-853-0044
E-mail sales@arcadiapublishing.com
For customer service and orders:
Toll-Free 1-888-313-2665

Visit us on the Internet at www.arcadiapublishing.com

DEDICATION

Dedicated with much love to my late grandmother, Eliza Salters,
to my late dear mother, Carrie Ora Dell Bright,
to my late aunt, Bama Stephens.
To my two living daughters, Kiara Migon and Karielle Eliza Stephens,
whose patience, confidence and love have helped me to
sustain hard times over the years. I love you all for your unselfish love.

CONTENTS

Acknowledgments   6

Preface   8

Introduction   10

1.   The Founding Years   13

2.   Dr. Dan and Williams Island   23

3.   Idlewild Lot Owners Association   31

4.   Religious Life and Services   37

5.   The Wilson Legacy   46

6.   The UNIA, Depression Years, and CCC Camp Number 1619   59

7.   The Heyday Entertainment Era   65

8.   The National Idlewilders Club, Inc   95

9.   Year Round Community Life   103

10. Economic Decline and Rebirth   119

Selected Bibliography and About the Author   128

ACKNOWLEDGMENTS

Like all living things, this book was made possible through the divine love and blessings of the Creator, my parents, my children, my African American and Ethnic Studies colleagues, and the professional staff of Michigan State University's Museum (MSUM), Michigan Humanities Council (MHC) and the Research Council of the University of Nebraska at Lincoln. To the staff of the following research repositories who have assisted me as I have traveled extensively and combed through hundreds of rare documents and photographs, I wish to especially thank: Paul Gifford, Associate Archivist, Genesee Historical Collections Center at University of Michigan-Flint Library; Mark Harvey, Reference Archivist of the Library of Michigan in East Lansing, Michigan; the staff of the Burton Historical Library in the main branch of the Detroit Public Library; the Carter G. Woodson Public Library in Chicago, Illinois; and the Library of Congress; Robin Van Fleet, Assistant Curator of the Manuscript Division of the Daniel Hale Williams Papers at Howard University's Moorland Spingard Library in Washington, D.C.; Linda Seidman, Head, Special Collections and Archives of the W. E. B. Du Bois Collection at the University of Massachusetts-Amherst; Samuel W. Black, Associate Curator for African American History, of the Charles W. Chesnutt Collection at the Western Reserve Historical Society in Cleveland, OH; James Hoffmann, Curator of the Photographic Division of the Marcus M. Garvey Collection at the Schomburg Center for Research on Black Culture in New York; Susan Dooley, Librarian of the Yates Township Public Library in Idlewild, Michigan; staff volunteers of Pathfinder Library in Baldwin, Michigan, and Susan Sutton, Coordinator of Visual Reference Services at the Indiana Historical Society in Indianapolis, Indiana. Some recognition must also go to the staff of the Grand Rapids Public Library, Alice Selfridge of Big Rapids Public Library, Debra Tucker of Wayne State University's Purdy/Kresge Library, the staff in the reference department at Indiana University-Bloomington Library, Sandra Shryock of the Maine Historical Society, Emily A. Herrick, Reference Librarian of the Maine Historical Library, and Signe Swanson, Reference Librarian at the University of Nebraska's Love Library for assisting me in retrieving important details from newspaper articles, general reference sources, and books on the subject. From the many traditional and non-traditional private collections I was privileged to see, use, and reproduce photographs from, thank you. From this list, I want to thank Dr. Nathaniel W. Leach, Archivist of Second Baptist Church of Detroit for sharing rare materials with me from the Reverend Robert L. Bradby Sr. collection, Ms. Maryellen Wilson of Evanston, Illinois and Mr. Herman O. Wilson, Jr. of Muskegon, Michigan for providing rare photographs and other materials on the Herman O. and Lela G. Wilson legacy in Idlewild, Ms. Carlean Gill of Saginaw, Michigan for sharing photographs on Arthur Braggs and the Arthur Braggs Idlewild Revue, Mrs. Cliniece Stubbs for connecting me with some of the entertainers who performed with the revue, and Mama Helen Curry, Mrs. Audrey Kathryn Bullett, President and Founder of Dawn's Light Centre, and Mrs. Mabel R. Williams of Idlewild, Michigan, and Ms. America

E. Nelson of Kalamazoo, Michigan for assisting with the recovery of local Idlewild history. To Mr. Julian Swain, Ms. Edith McCauley, Mrs. Minnie Murphy, and Ms. Arnell Pugh (also known as Najwa I Um'Rani) of the Chicago and Rock Island, Illinois areas, I wish to especially thank each of you for assisting me during the last hours of my work to collect photographs. To you, Edith, I am indebted for the long hours of work you devoted to this project. To Mrs. Dotty Rose of Detroit, Michigan, I want to thank you for all the encouragement, assistance, guidance, and confidence you gave me, and to Mr. Conklin Bray and Ms. Gabrielle Greene of Detroit, thank you for sharing the Reverends H. Franklin Bray and Robert L. Bradby materials and stories with me. Without the unselfish support from each of you this project would not have been completed.

This book would also not be possible without the support and encouragement of several individuals who unselfishly gave their time, energy, and expertise. On the top of this list, I want to gratefully acknowledge Mr. Brendan McKenna, Acquisitions Editor of Arcadia Publishing, for believing in this project; to my dear colleague and best friend, Dr. Venetria K. Patton, I want to thank you for your comments and suggestions and for critically reading my work repeatedly and offering significant recommendations. To Mr. Paul Lee, Director of Best Efforts, Inc., Ruth Lewis and Carolyn Schofield, each independent researchers, whose openness, honesty, and high intellectual standards served as important sources of encouragement and inspiration, thank you. While researching and preparing this manuscript, it would also not have been possible to secure important details without the support of Mrs. Ann Walters of the *Lake County Star* newspaper, Mrs. Susan Dooley of the Yates Township Public Library, Chris Wilson of the Henry Ford Museum, and many other individuals in Idlewild, including Mr. John O. Meeks, Owner of Morton Motel, President Emeritus of the Mid-Michigan Idlewilders, and founder of the African-American Idlewild Chamber of Commerce, Mabel R. Williams, founder, Idlewild Historical Museum and Cultural Center, Mrs. Gladys Chipchase and Francelle Morrow of Chicago, and other individuals in other parts of Illinois and Michigan whom I have had consistent contact with in pursuit of answers to some complex questions. I also want to extend a sincere appreciation to Dr. Richard Lonsdale, Professor Emeritus, Department of Geography, University of Nebraska-Lincoln, for suggesting that I employ a geographical angle to my work. Thank you for recommending that I contact Dr. John Fraser Hart, Professor, Department of Geography, University of Minnesota, whose valuable field study on the community was extremely useful. The documentation and rare photographs of Idlewild you shared that were based on your 40- year plus original field research in 1959 were truly appreciated.

It is equally important to recognize other support mechanisms and individuals that labored with me while traveling and conducting research. I am so thankful for the financial support I received from my work with Michigan State University Museum (MSUM). Thank you so very much Drs. Laurie Sommers, now at Georgia State University, Marsha McDowell, Kurt Dewhurst and Yvonne Lockwood for hiring and encouraging me to put my best foot forward as an independent contractor for the Michigan Traditional Arts Program. The preliminary work I completed while employed with MSUM and the collaborative projects we worked on together have helped in many ways to pave the way for this book. Next, special thanks goes to the Research Council of UNL for funding several small grants to support my travels and the costs to reproduce most of the photographs included in this book. However, without the support of the Michigan Humanities Council, this book and the traveling photographic exhibition that accompanies this book would not have been possible. Finally, some recognition must be given to the faculty of the African-American and African Studies Program, the Institute for Ethnic Studies, and the Department of Anthropology and Geography of the University of Nebraska at Lincoln for supporting my research.

Of course this book does not represent a comprehensive photographic treatment of residential life in Idlewild, Michigan. However, I would hope readers will find it a worthy source of information, inspiration, and encouragement in the pursuit of understanding more about the people and community of Idlewild.

PREFACE

Segregation was a way of life in the first half of 20th century America. The impact of such was made so clear when the famous African-American scholar, Dr. W. E. B. Du Bois, declared that the problem of the century would be the problem of the color line. As long as legal racial segregation existed, African Americans would be forced and motivated to build and operate their own communities. The story of Idlewild, like that of so many other African-American resort communities in the United States, provides a real life example of how Black Americans struggled to achieve equality in a country that, although founded on human and civil rights and Democratic principles, remained much delayed in practicing them. Idlewild is a town that, over a period of eighty seven years, has experienced the seeds of creation, growth in leaps and bounds with a significant peak in popularity and population size between 1929 and 1959, a period of economic decline in the 1960s and 1970s, new developments in the 1980s, and rebirth throughout the 1990s.

Located in rural Western Michigan, Idlewild has a year-round population of 784 residents. Racial and demographic factors were important to Idlewild's early development, as well as its economic decline and rebirth from 1965 to 1990. Although the Idlewild community was once known as the largest and most famous of African-American resort communities in the United States, it is now a retirement and family community in search of a new identity. Recent data obtained from the 1990 U.S. Census, for example, reveals that of the 784 residents who live in Idlewild, which is located in Yates Township, year round, 74.3 percent or 510 persons of that population are African American, and 274 of them are of European ancestry. However, these figures do not provide the most accurate accounting of the total population in the community. Township officials estimate the number of seasonal residents, who are primarily African Americans, to be approximately 5,000, bringing the total summer population to 5,784 from May to September.

This book gives voice to these year round, seasonal, and former citizens in the Idlewild, Michigan community through visual imagery and textual analysis. For far too long these citizens have had little influence and/or control over the documentation of their lived experiences. However, this book is essentially a collaborative history of the community that grew out of my personal relationship with members of the community and my desire to work with them and to curate a photographic exhibit that would assist in the development of a historical museum and cultural center in Idlewild. The book comes as a direct result of a participatory, emancipatory, and collaborative initiative.

My interest in Idlewild began with a series of in-depth interviews and conversations with local leaders and residents in the community during the summer of 1993, in which they shared stories about the history of the community, economic decay and development in the community, and their feelings about community-university coalition building. While employed as an independent contractor for Michigan State University Museum (MSUM) from 1993 to 1996, I interviewed over 50 residents in the community, and identified four credible and respected sources in the community to be collaborators. These individuals include Mabel R. Williams, president of the Lake County Merrymaker's (LCMM), Friend of Historic Idlewild (FHI), and member of the Lake County Enterprising Zone Commission (LCEZC); Audrey K. Bullett, former Yates Township Supervisor, lay historian, poet, and community activist, and secretary of the National Idlewild Lot Owners Association (ILOA); John Meeks, Owner, Morton Motel, and founder of the Mid-Michigan Idlewilders, and the Idlewild African American Chamber of Commerce; and Mary Trucks, Executive Director of FiveCAP, Inc., the lead agency for the Lake County Enterprising Zone Commission.

The opportunity to establish a personal relationship with these local leaders was critical to my overcoming one of the problems of being viewed as an outsider. One major benefit of establishing close relations with these leaders, and maintaining contacts with year-round and seasonal residents, was my gaining "insider" access to information about the extensive amount of community history and the kinds of services provided. A second major benefit concerned my role and participation in a negotiated collaboration with these community leaders and residents that ensured positive results regarding the planning, implementation, and completion of several projects. Essentially, what these interviews revealed was that there was a need to facilitate a community-building project that would create a community-university partnership and encourage concrete changes as a result of several systematic community-based research (CBR) projects.

The benefits of CBR were realized when these four community leaders-collaborators expressed an interest in developing and promoting the rich musical, narrative, and cultural history and heritage of Idlewild. After several meetings with these leaders for the purpose of assisting them in meeting their goals, a detailed plan to write a grant for a traveling photographic exhibition that would give the community greater visibility with its revitalization efforts, including a means to attract visitors, and a strategy to improve the facilities that would permanently house the exhibit and other cultural events, was established. As such, it was my objective and responsibility as a community-based researcher to assist the community in the fulfillment of some of its goals. However, the projects outlined and completed also allowed me to link my social practice to my scholarly research interests in the Idlewild community. The first project came in the form of a proposal that received $16,500 in funding from the Michigan Humanities Council (MHC) to create the traveling photographic exhibition that documents community and family narrative traditions by highlighting past, present and future possibilities of Idlewild. Project collaborators included five members of the Michigan State University Museum (MSUM) staff, two Idlewild community stakeholders, and myself. Additional funding and support were sought through a series of smaller funded grant proposals from the Research Council of the University of Nebraska-Lincoln. However, this project developed as an oral history project that would increase institutional and individual interest in the humanities and in African-American communities. A third project, which was submitted two times to the National Endowment for the Humanities (NEH) Collaborative Research Division, entailed the collection, documentation, and analysis of oral histories, and also the instruction for members of the Idlewild community to do basic ethnographic field research so that they can record the history of their community. An advisory board, consisting of three university professors and four community members, was formed to avoid "fragmented" collaborations in the pursuit of this and other future projects. This book represents one aspect of the initial project resulting from this community-university partnership.

In the pursuit of these projects, I witnessed a few conflicts between and within certain groups in the community and several funding agencies while these CBR projects were in the planning stages. Witnessing many accomplishments and disappointments, I remained confident, focused, determined, and supportive of everyone involved in the research project as community members resolved their individual conflicts, and as I continuously worked to fulfill my scholarly obligations. By understanding the intersection of rural and urban lifestyles and values, I was able to circumvent issues of ownership, cultural rights, and inclusion, all issues addressed by community members, not to mention, the responsibilities of being a solid researcher in the academy. Because CBR complements the self-interests of the community and the researcher, it was important

9

that my ideas, skills, and talents were being used for good effects. Consequently, in the process of strengthening and showcasing the unique history of this remote community through the establishment of a professional local and regional cultural program, I needed to link this local history to my scholarship.

While conducting in-depth interviews with seasonal, former, and year-round residents, I discovered significant stories imbedded in the interviews that would make for a compelling subject of research. These stories reveal important information about collective memories and folkloric constructions of community by year-round, former, and seasonal Idlewilders. These stories were a means for all citizens to retain strong ties to Idlewild's past. These stories are presented in this book through my collection of photographs obtained by past and present, and seasonal and year round residents of the community. Because a growing body of cases illustrate that "CBR is not only good science, but often produces more useful, action-oriented results for the communities that participate in CBR projects," it was my goal to not only develop a publication record, but also to give legitimacy to my service in the community, and to use research as a tool to affect social change.

INTRODUCTION

This book illustrates why the community of Idlewild continues to be recognized as one of the oldest, most famous, and most memorable African-American resort communities in the United States. During the second decade of the 20th century, a small yet clearly distinguishable African American middle class had been established in several urban centers. Like many urbanites, they wanted the opportunity for recreational pursuits, but in a setting far removed from racism and discrimination in the cities. Because Northwest Michigan represented a likely location to establish a resort for African Americans, four white land developers and their wives organized the Idlewild Resort Company (IRC). Erastus Branch and his wife, Flora, and Adelbert Branch and his wife, Isabelle, from White Cloud, Michigan, and Wilbur M. Lemon and his wife, Mayme, and A.E. Wright and his wife, Modolin, of Chicago, organized IRC during the pre-World War I era.

No one knows who designated the name of the community; however, one folk saying suggests it refers to idle men and wild women. Whatever the circumstances, IRC organized its first excursion to attract African American professionals from Michigan, Illinois, Indiana, and other Midwestern states to tour the rustic community. One prominent personality to relocate to Idlewild was Dr. Daniel Hale Williams who, in 1893 became the first surgeon in the United States to perform open-heart surgery. Dr. Dan, as he was to be later called in Idlewild, Herman O. and Lela G. Wilson of Chicago, and twenty-three others were among the first group of African Americans to join IRC's excursion. By 1919 a pamphlet was developed to promote the community entitled "Beautiful Idlewild," which described Idlewild as "the hunter's paradise," a place renowned "for its beautiful lakes of pure spring water" and "its myriads of game fish."

IRC sold much of their land to Dr. Dan and Louis B. Anderson of Chicago, and Robert Riffe and William Green of Cleveland, who collaboratively formed the Idlewild Improvement Association (IIA). IIA sold property to such notables as NAACP co-founder, Dr. W.E.B. Du Bois, cosmetic entrepreneur Madame C.J. Walker, Lemuel L. Foster, president of Fisk University, and the famous African-American novelist Charles W. Chesnutt. IIA was also responsible for recruiting other professionals such as William Pickens, field secretary of the NAACP, Reverend H. Franklin Bray, and his wife, Virginia Bray, who together founded the first formal church in Idlewild, and the Reverend Robert L. Bradby, Sr. of Second Baptist Church of Detroit, and Irene McCoy Gaines who were instrumental in the development of the Idlewild Lot Owners Association (ILOA).

Idlewild, by then known throughout the United States as the Black Eden of Michigan, had become one of the few places African Americans could find peace of mind, and could escape systematic practices of racism and discrimination. As this black intelligentsia developed Idlewild, some relocated as activists and members of Marcus Mosiah Garvey's Universal Negro Improvement Association (UNIA), some as followers of Du Bois' National Association for the Advancement of Colored People (NAACP), others as believers of the late Booker T. Washington's political machine, and others as potential investors. However, for the majority of these families, the idea of land ownership conveyed social status.

Idlewild quickly became the intellectual center for economic development and racial progress in North America during the pre-World War II era. The ILOA, for example, had become a national organization with members from over thirty-four states. In addition, the Purple Palace, Paradise Clubhouse and the Idlewild Clubhouse provided summer entertainment for tourists and employment opportunities for seasonal and year round residents in the community. However, Idlewild during the post-World War II era attracted a new African-American "working" middle class. With the construction of a few paved roads and the greater availability of the automobile, a new generation of Black entrepreneurs began to invest in Idlewild. Phil Giles and Arthur Braggs took advantage of the market by developing The Flamingo Club and The Paradise Club, which featured well-known entertainers such as Della Reese, Al Hibbler, Bill Doggett, Jackie Wilson, T-Bone Walker, George Kirby, The Four Tops, Roy Hamilton, Brooks Benton, Choker Campbell, Lottie "the Body" Tatum-Graves, the Rhythm Kings, the Harlem Brothers, the Dyerettes, and many other performers, who entertained thousands of Idlewilders and white citizens in neighboring Lake County townships throughout the 1950s and early 1960s.

With the passing of the Civil Rights Act of 1964, the many rebellions that followed in 1968, the Vietnam War, and a national recession in the early 1970s, and the inability of seasonal business owners in Idlewild to be competitive with other vacation outlets in the United States, the community suffered a significant social and economic loss. The children of many of the original families who were born in the community were now forced to relocate to other cities in Michigan, Illinois, and elsewhere to find suitable employment to care for their families. As the community underwent a significant population decline, Idlewild became a lesser-known family vacation community. However, in the 1980s, an increasing number of new retirees, many who visited the area during its prime, relocated to the community and launched an intensive revitalization effort. Township officials organized a planning commission, zoning board, and other in-group initiatives as a way to encourage community input and to offer solutions to improve the community. Community Development Block Grants (CDBG) were obtained for demolition, additional roadwork, and other structural changes, which eventually resulted in a complete, make over of the Island.

While the population began to increase, it continued to do so through a disproportionate number of retirees, which placed a heavy burden on seasonal residents to pay for community facilities and services for year around homeowners with limited incomes. By the early 1990s, the community's attention was turned away from building projects and turned toward the renovation of existing township properties and increasing community pride among all citizens. Although these pragmatic developments were taking place, the community continued to suffer economically. However, the community's vision for social change was partially fulfilled when the federal government designated Lake County, Michigan, as an Enterprising Community, which led to the installation of a sewer system and natural gas. Today, Idlewild is well on its way to revitalizing community life for its residents.

The thematic focus of this book explores the community of Idlewild as a recreational haven for African Americans. Chapter one highlights the founding years of Idlewild's history, the contributions of the IRC, and the role of the founding families and many early black settlers. Chapter two traces the presence of Dr. Daniel Hale Williams and his IIA. Chapter three summarizes the contributions of the ILOA, documenting its origins, purpose, leaders, and their many achievements. Chapter four highlights the role of various religious institutions in the community, including the founding of the first church, The People's Community Tabernacle Church. Chapter five details the legacy of the Wilson's, including the building of the famous Paradise Club, Paradise Hotel, and Wilson's Grocery.

Chapter six explores the history of radicalism in Idlewild during the Great Depression era as well as the activities of President Roosevelt's Civilian Conservation Corp, and the Universal Negro Improvement Association and African Communities League in the community. Chapter seven focuses on the heyday entertainment era in Idlewild with Phil Giles' famous Flamingo Club and Arthur Braggs' Idlewild Revue at the Paradise Club. Chapter eight outlines the establishment of and continued presence of the National Idlewilders' Club, Inc. Chapter nine focuses on year round community life in Idlewild. Chapter ten traces rebirth in the community, including the contributions of FiveCAP, Inc. Michigan State University Extension, the Lake County Enterprise Zone Board, the Idlewild Historical Museum and Cultural Center, and other organizations.

Although Idlewild's tourism has significantly declined, African Americans throughout the United States maintain strong ties to the community through frequent visits and their involvement in the National Idlewilders' annual celebrations. In addition, the National Lot Owners Association with local chapters in eight cities, contributes to the community's significance. The memories of year-round, seasonal, and former Idlewild residents and visitors who now live throughout the United States and abroad are evidence of the continuing significance of the community.

One

THE FOUNDING YEARS

At the beginning of the century, there was a tremendous rise in new economic and social opportunities in the U.S. for African Americans. Because resort facilities across the country were segregated, in 1912 four white couples purchased a 2,700-acre parcel of land and secured land rights for two sections near Idlewild Lake in rural Michigan to establish a vacation community for African Americans. The Idlewild Resort Company (IRC), the organization that founded the community, consisted of William E. Sanders, president; Albert Flogaus, secretary; Wilbur M. Lemon and his wife, Mayme E. Lemon; A. E. Wright and his wife, Modolin M. Wright; Erasteus G. Branch and his wife, Flora Branch; and Adelbert Branch and his wife, Isabella Branch. Believing that northwest Michigan would appeal to African Americans, IRC promoted the sale of land to residents of Gary, Indiana and Chicago. This brought a number of African Americans to the area, some of which helped to develop property in the region. IRC hired black real estate men from Chicago who advertised lots in a black Chicago newspaper for $1 down and $1 a month. IRC also built cottages, Doghouses, and the Idlewild Clubhouse on and near the Island. With the erection of these structures, Idlewild quickly gained a national reputation as a hunter's paradise and as a place renowned for its beautiful lakes of pure spring water and game fish.

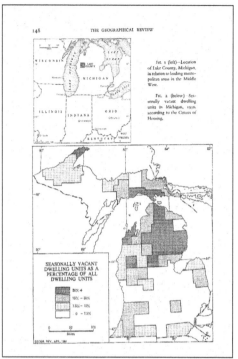

This is a map of Michigan with Idlewild, Traverse City, Grand Rapids, Lansing, Saginaw, and Detroit shown. (Courtesy of Dr. John Fraser Hart, Professor, Department of Geography, University of Minnesota, with permission from Peter Lewis of the Geographical Society.)

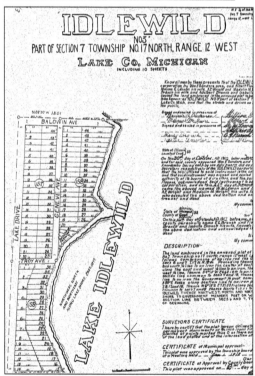

These are Plats 2 and 3 of Williams Island and Lake Idlewild. (Courtesy of the Lake County Historical Society.)

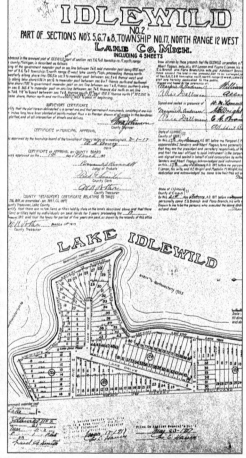

Mrs. Helen Buckles and her husband journeyed four days from Medicnehat, Canada, to the 1915 Chicago World Fair and purchased the first plot of land on sale in Idlewild. Mr. and Mrs. Buckles were the first couple to spend the night in Idlewild. In 1916 they lived six months in a tool shed while waiting for their promised home to be finished. (Courtesy of Susan Dooley, Yates Township Public Library.)

Harry Branch's residence is to the right of the office of the Idlewild Resort Company and Museum in Idlewild, in this photograph from c. 1933. (Courtesy of JoAnne Branch Queen, grand daughter of Harry Branch, one of the founders of IRC.)

Shown here is the back view of the Idlewild Historical Museum, c. 1933. (Courtesy of JoAnne Branch Queen.)

This photograph is an interior view of the Idlewild Historical Museum, c. 1933. (Courtesy of JoAnne Branch Queen.)

Excursion groups were organized from various Midwestern cities to visit Idlewild. More than 300 people traveled from Indianapolis, from which a bus was purchased and used to promote these trips to Idlewild, *c.* 1933. Others traveled by train. (Courtesy of JoAnne Branch Queen.)

This excursion group is shown riding horses taken in front of the IRC office, *c.* 1933. (Courtesy of JoAnne Branch Queen.)

This is an official IRC Certificate, from *c.* 1935. (Courtesy of the State Archives of Michigan.)

JoAnne Branch Queen is shown standing on the dock, while resorters are having fun in Lake Idlewild, *c.* 1933. (Courtesy of JoAnne Branch Queen.)

Here, an excursion group stands on a dock, from c. 1933. (Courtesy of JoAnne Branch Queen.)

This excursion group appears to be quite thrilled about Idlewild, while posing near a bus close to the IRC office, c. 1933. (Courtesy of JoAnne Branch Queen.)

In this photograph, a group poses while visiting Idlewild, *c.* 1933. (Courtesy of JoAnne Branch Queen.)

Religious groups often held baptisms in the lake. This picture captures a Tabernacle Baptism in Lake Idlewild, *c.* 1933. (Courtesy of Conklin Bray.)

This is the White Cloud office of IRC, which was under the leadership of Rollo Branch, son of Harry Branch. This image is from c. 1933. (Courtesy of JoAnne Branch Queen.)

IRC also sold property to Black land purchasers in Woodland Park in Bitely, Michigan, establishing a smaller Black resort just 20 miles from Idlewild. Shown here is the Flossia and Lucia cottage in Woodland Park. (Courtesy of the Yates Township Public Library.)

THE DOGHOUSES

In search of relief for his wife's hay fever, Dr. Ernest T. Cox from Columbus, Ohio, decided to investigate the climate in Idlewild, Michigan. This was to be the beginning of a yearly trek for this family's four generations of summer residents to the popular resort. Anxious to reap the benefits of Michigan's atmosphere, Mary Ellen Cox and a friend packed up their two respective toddlers and headed for Idlewild by train—a 16-hour trip at that time with layovers in Chicago and Grand Rapids. The two mothers found accommodations on the Island in two of the many identical-one room "doghouses," so called because of their resemblance to the structures. These little cottages, about 30 in number were lined up in a curve along the north side of the Island. There was a long narrow boardwalk in front of the houses extending from the first to the last. The cottages had a front door opening onto the boardwalk, and a window at the opposite end facing little Lake Idlewild. Each cottage contained two cots, a mash stand (complete with pitcher and bowl), a bucket for carrying water from the public hand pump located behind the center of the board walk (in a park-like area), and a kerosene heater to take the chill off on cool days. A small stereo appliance was used for making a cup of tea, and other hot drinks. Occupants were served hot tasty meals in the dining room of the Idlewild Clubhouse on the south side of the Island overlooking the lake. Toilet facilities were primitive (out-houses, as they were called) located far behind the Doghouses near the first and last building. There was one for ladies and one for men.

Pictured are some of the Doghouses. These 25 10 by 12 sleeping cottages were built by the Idlewild Resort Company. (From the collection of Dawn's Light Centre, Inc.)

Two

DR. DAN AND WILLIAM'S ISLAND

The first distinguished group of African-American professionals to tour Idlewild came in 1915 during the first Idlewild Resort Company excursion. Although rapid development of the community did not occur until after World War I, the presence of several highly respected African-American community members such as Dr. Daniel Hale Williams helped to increase the population size. The founders believed that Idlewild represented an important site in creating what Alain Locke (1925) defined as the age of the "New Negro."

Dr. Williams, who in 1893 became the first surgeon in the U.S. to perform open-heart surgery, purchased nearly 27 acres of land and built a sub-division, known as The Oakmere. "Dr. Dan," as he was known throughout Idlewild, sold lots to such notables as NAACP co-founder, Dr. W. E. B. Du Bois, cosmetic giant Madame C.J. Walker, the famous African-American novelist Charles Waddell Chesnutt, and many others. Dr. Dan and his associates from Chicago and Cleveland organized the Idlewild Improvement Association (IIA), which paved the way for a variety of professional services and businesses to the community, including nightclubs, a post office, barber shops, medical services, grocery stores, a roller rink, filling stations, senior citizen housing, automobile repair shops, and police and fire protection to Idlewild. Officers of the Idlewild Improvement Association (IIA) were Dr. Daniel Hale Williams (president), Robert H. Riffe and William R. Green of Cleveland, and Dave Manson (treasurer) and Louis B. Anderson (secretary) of Chicago. This development represented an important period in Idlewild's history, since IRC and IIA merged, and the last Idlewild Plat Number Eight was recorded on June 25, 1926. IIA took over the activities of IRC, and continued to develop the Island with a host of new buildings.

Dr. Daniel Hale Williams was president of the Idlewild Improvement Association. Before retiring from a distinguished career as founder and chief surgeon of Provident Hospital in Chicago, Dr. Daniel Hale Williams purchased property and made his permanent residence in Idlewild on Lake Drive. (From the Daniel Hale Williams Papers, Courtesy of Howard University's Moorland Spingard Research Collection.)

The Oakmere Hotel and sleeping cottages accommodated two hundred guests. The Oakmere had electricity, shower baths, and was modern in all respects for the 1920s. (Courtesy of the State Archives of Michigan.)

This is a lakeside view of the Idlewild Clubhouse. The Clubhouse, center of activity in the early 1920s, was located on the Island. The facility was built by IRC and developed by the Idlewild Improvement Company. The clubhouse had modern dinning room services. It was being leased to Mr. and Mrs. Carl W. Jenkins of Cleveland, Ohio. The menu included steak, chicken, and fish dinners, and lunch served at all hours. Special parties, cafeteria services, and other occasions were provided as well. Food supplies were purchased locally from merchants in the Village of Baldwin, and from farmers in the surrounding areas. (Courtesy of the State Archives of Michigan.)

This is the roadway and parking in front of the Idlewild Club House. Dr. Dan died at his Oakmere home on August 4, 1931. Mr. and Mrs. Virgil L. Williams became the new owners of the Idlewild Club House, Purple Palace, and Oakmere Hotel. When they turned over the hotel and the Club House, Phil Giles built the Phil Giles Flamingo Club, renovated the hotel, and called it the Phil Giles Hotel. By the late 1940s, the Clubhouse had been converted and became Polk's Skating Rink. (From the private collection of Maryellen Wilson.)

Shown here is the footbridge to the Island. The Island was connected to the mainland first by footbridges and later by roadway. (Courtesy of the State Archives of Michigan.)

In this scene, children perform a mock wedding in the large lobby of the clubhouse, in front of the large brick fireplace, with parents looking on to the right in the doorway entrance. Identified in the photograph are Sonny Bundle, Harrison Gaines, Jack Davidson, Clyde Timmons, Ann Hawkins, and McAllister J. Merchant Jr. (Courtesy of Alpheus Merchant.)

This is the deed to the property owned by Lelia Walker Wilson, daughter of Madame C.J. Walker, the millionaire cosmetics entrepreneur, who purchased the land one year following the death of her mother. (Courtesy of the Indiana Historical Library.)

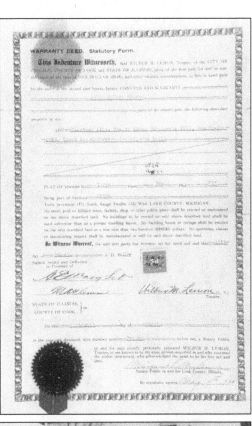

Resorters who migrated inwardly to Idlewild adopted one of three prevailing ideologies: the accomodationists, who were followers of Booker T. Washington, president of the Tuskegee Institute and Normal School; integrationists, who embraced the philosophy of Dr. Du Bois, who was the editor of the *Crisis* for the NAACP; and the nationalists, who were influenced by Marcus Mosiah Garvey. Garvey was the President-General of the Universal Negro Improvment Association and African Communities League. Pictured on horse is Booker T. Washington posing on the campus of the Tuskegee Institute, in Tuskegee, Alabama. (International Press, Courtesy of the Library of Congress.)

Dr. W.E.B. Du Bois (on the right) is shown in this photograph taken in Idlewild in 1920. A 1921 *Crisis* magazine article followed, which put Idlewild in the national spotlight. In it, Dr. Du Bois who was one of the leading black intellectuals and social critics of the day, describes the commercial potential in and aesthetic beauty of Idlewild for African-American investors in the following manner:

For sheer physical beauty—for sheen of water and golden air, for nobleness of tree and flower of shrub, for shining river and song of bird and the low, moving whisper of sun, moon, and star, it is the beautifulest stretch I have seen for twenty years; and then to that add fellowship—sweet, strong women and keen-witted men from Canada and Texas, California and New York, Ohio, Missouri and Illinois—all sons and great-grandchildren of Ethiopia, all with the wide leisure of rest and play—can you imagine a more marvelous thing than Idlewild?

(From the W.E.B. Du Bois Library at the University of Massachusetts Amherst.)

Charles Chesnutt is shown here with grandson, Johhny Slade. (From the private collection of Johhny Slade.)

This photograph is of Louis B. Anderson. (From the collection of the Illinois State Historical Library.)

Robert H. Riffe came to Idlewild on July 20, 1920. A realtor, Riffe made financial contributions to the ILOA construction fund, which was named in his honor, the Robert Riffe Youth Center. (Courtesy of the National ILOA.)

Pictured with Dr. Du Bois and Walter White is William Pickens, Secretary of the NAACP during a group posing at one of the annual NAACP meetings in Washington D.C. This photograph was taken one month prior to Picken's visit to Idlewild during one of the community's annual Chautauqua. Writing about the event in the September 16, 1927 issue of *The Detroit Independent*, Pickens observed the following during the Chautauqua event in 1927:

> *Dr. Robert L Bradby asked for a show of hands as he called the roll of the states. Many states, north, south, east and west, answered, the roll call—the greatest number of hands being shown for Illinois, Michigan, and Ohio. Others were there from as far west as Kansas and Nebraska, as far south as Alabama, and Texas, as far east as New England and New York, and as far north as Toronto, Canada. People from the east often drive to Buffalo, then take Lake Erie steamer to Detroit, and then drive on to Idlewild. But the resort can be reached by railroad, via Grand Rapids (pg. 5). (Courtesy of the Library of Congress.)*

Reverend Robert L. Bradby Sr. pictured in front of his cottage in Idlewild, c. 1937. (From the Angela Bradby and Gabrielle Bradby Greene Historical Collection.)

Three

IDLEWILD LOT OWNERS' ASSOCIATION

IRC also founded the Idlewild Lot Owners Association (ILOA) in the state of Illinois in 1921, which was incorporated in the state of Michigan in 1932. ILOA celebrates its 80th anniversary this year. The mission and goals of ILOA are to maintain an association of all persons interested in the welfare and improvement of the community of Idlewild by promoting positive environmental, social, and humanitarian issues of concern to property owners. A national organization consisting of property owners in such areas as Detroit, Chicago, Cleveland, Indiana, and St. Louis, ILOA is a non-profit, charitable, service, recreational, civic, and welfare organization. ILOA now has local chapters in these regions. As part of its tradition, ILOA regularly sponsors a variety of summer programs for youth, and adult activities (an annual fashion flair and amateur show), to encourage cultural heritage and pride within the community. From the late 1920s to the present, ILOA has been a leader in the Idlewild community. Past presidents include Irene McCoy Gaines of Chicago, Reverend Robert L. Bradby, Sr. of Detroit, Sulee Stinson of Detroit, Margot Harding of Chicago, and Ann Hawkins of Chicago.

ILOA's annual Fashion Flair event, which is accompanied by a program booklet, takes place each year during Idlewilder's Week. The amateur show used professionals and volunteers representing various member chapters of ILOA and the National Idlewilder's Club to preserve these traditions by showcasing local and regional talents and entertainment. Gladys Chipchase organized the Fashion Flair, while Maw and Paw Longhorn, all of Chicago, organized the amateur shows.

This is a group of ILOA members
during a meeting in the early 1960s,
at the Robert Riffe Youth Center,
Lot Owner's Association Clubhouse
in Idlewild, Michigan. (From the
collection of Mrs. Vivian Logan.)

From c. 1940 to 1950, Gladys Chipchase
consulted Ms. Desiree Pybuyn of Chicago
to help organize, as well as serve as the
commentator for the ILOA fashion shows.
Ms. Pybuyn had worked with professional
models in fashion shows in Chicago,
and when she traveled to Idlewild she
brought some of them with her to produce
top-notch fashion shows in the community.
Charles Douglass, another commentator
from Chicago, served ILOA after Desiree.
(Courtesy of Mrs. Gladys Chipchase.)

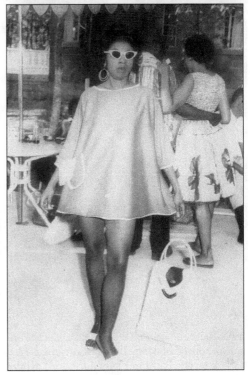

This is a collage of Maryellen Wilson
modeling in the 1950s during one of
the ILOA's Fashion Flairs on the patio
of the Eagle's Nest and in the Lot
Owners' Clubhouse. (From the private
collection of Maryellen Wilson.)

Gladys Chipchase gives an award to Irene McCoy Gaines during the annual Lot Owners' amateur show. (Courtesy of Gladys Chipchase.)

In this collage of Maryellen Wilson, she is seen modeling two different outfits during one of the ILOA's recent Fashion Flairs during Idlewilder's Week. (Courtesy of Denise Bellamy.)

Jess Brown, president of the Mid-Michigan Idlewilders, Inc. is seen posing during one of ILOA's fashion shows. (Courtesy of Denise Bellamy.)

In this scene, Idlewidlers are seen celebrating during one of the 50s-plus annual celebrations during Idlewilders' Week. The 50-plus celebrations, which are organized by Mrs. Mildred Kyles of Detroit, are held in the Lot Owners' Clubhouse. (Courtesy of Denise Bellamy.)

Freddie Mitchell, Lillie Smith, and Denise Bellamy get their picture taken during one of the 50-plus dinner affairs held in the Idlewild Lot Owner's Association Clubhouse. (Courtesy of Denise Bellamy.)

In 1999, the Mid-Michigan Idlewilders brought the nationally reknowned Contours to Idlewild, who performed in the ILOA clubhouse. (Courtesy of Denise Bellamy.)

Four

RELIGIOUS LIFE
AND SERVICES

At first there was one main church in the community of Idlewild, known as the People's Community Church of Christ, which was founded, built, and pastored by the Reverend Harry Franklin Bray. He and his bride, Mrs. Virginia Bray, came to Idlewild in 1922, where he found relief from asthma and formed a religious program for others at the Island Clubhouse. Prior to this development, Mrs. Lela G. Wilson and Mother Mary L. Turner held Christian services in their homes respectively.

However, when the Reverend elected to settle in Idlewild permanently, Edward Elsner (husband of the community's first post-mistress) helped to raise $500 to purchase the four lots needed to build a rustic structure. Additional lots were also donated by Mr. Herman O. Wilson and Mr. Branch. At the time the church was a tent with sand for the floor. It was the only erected house of worship in the community. Later, it became a structure for those who lived in Idlewild year-round, and for those lot owners and their friends who were coming in increasing numbers from Detroit, Chicago, Cleveland, Indianapolis, and other urban areas. The Tabernacle, the Mother Church of Idlewild, was first called the People's Community Church of Christ, and it served as a non-denominational worship service. In 1928, snow collapsed the building and services were held in the basement. By 1929, the church's membership had grown, the facilities needed improving, and a second structure was built by Oscar Blankenship, John Simmons, Herman O. Wilson, Charles Scott, and many others. The formal opening of the new "Idlewild Community Tabernacle" took place in August 1929, with Michigan governor Fred Greene as the guest speaker. Famous African-American businessmen and women and others were present during the occasion.

Reverend H. Franklin Bray wearing his hat. (Courtesy of the Idlewild Tabernacle AME Church under the leadership of Reverend Stanley and Mrs. Sims.)

The People's Community Church of Christ (also known as the Tent) was founded by Reverend H. Franklin and Mrs. Virginia Bray in 1923. (Courtesy of Idlewild Tabernacle AME Church under the leadership of Reverend Stanley and Mrs. Sims.)

This is a photograph of the Community Tabernacle Church on Founder's Day at the Tabernacle, August 1929. The church structure was built in 1929 by Oscar Blankenship, a local contractor, from materials finished by the A. H. Broft Lumber Company of Baldwin, Michigan. (From the private collection of Dawn Light's Centre, Inc.)

Michigan Republican Governor Fred Greene (center) and his wife (right) are seen leaving the newly constructed Tabernacle Church in 1929 following a speech he delivered on Founder's Day during the dedication ceremony. Reverend Bray is seen standing in front of the governor as members of his congregation look on. (Courtesy of Ruth Odell.)

Idlewild Community Herald

Monthly News Magazine

Volume XII   JULY 1939   *Number 4*

BISHOP GREGG CAPTURES IDLEWILD

Accompanied by his wife, Dr. William H. Peck and Presiding Elder Washington, Bishop John A. Gregg of the Fourth Episcopal District of the African Methodist Church, arrived in Idlewild on Saturday, June 10, to be the guest of Rev. H. Franklin Bray and the Tabernacle, for what proved to be a most delightful and profitable visit.

On Sunday morning, although the clouds hung low and the rain poured, the spacious Tabernacle was well filled with a large and receptive audience to which at 11:00 a. m., the Bishop delivered one of the finest and most inspiring sermons ever heard from that national pulpit. Using as his text 1 John 4:8, "God is Love," the Bishop preached such a sermon on Love as stirred the hearts of all his hearers and moved them to a larger and clearer conception of who God is. There were times during the sermon when the Bishop rose to great heights of

THREE GENERATIONS OF A GREAT FAMILY

There is represented in the above picture of Mrs. R. L. Bradby, her daughter Catherine Smith, and her granddaughter, Beverly Smith, three generations of one of the finest, best qualified and most useful families in this or any other race group. Dr. Bradby has for more than a quarter of a century occupied the pulpit and developed the pastorate of the Second Baptist Church of Detroit, during which

The *Idlewild Community Herald* was designated as the official organ of the People's Community Church of Christ, Idlewild Community Center, and Idlewild Lot Owner's Association. It was published as a monthly news magazine by the Community Publishing Company. Reverend H. Franklin Bray was the editor and Susie J. Banton was contributing editor. Later, Irene McCoy Gaines, Elsie Roxborough, and Richard M. Hughes (Educational Director of the Houghton CCC Camp) became contributing associate editors. The *Idlewild Community Herald* was established in April of 1923 and admitted by the U.S. Postal Department as a second-class mailing by October of 1927. Publication of the *Herald* ceased shortly after the Idlewild Lot Owners' Association became the chief agency in 1939 after the death of Reverend Bray. ILOA was responsible for management of the magazine when it voted the organization could not afford to continue to produce it. (Courtesy of Mrs. Farina Davis.)

This is the Tabernacle AME Church as it appeared *c.* 1964. The Community Tabernacle Church was turned over to the Michigan AME Conference on August 30, 1939. The old church was moved from its original location to its present location in 1963. The original building was bricked over after this move. This was considered one of the largest moving jobs in Lake County since many of the original houses in the Village of Marlborough were moved into the Village of Baldwin at the turn of the century. (From the private collection of Dawn's Light Centre, Inc.)

Reverend Bray can be seen sitting on the front porch of his first house. (Courtesy of Conklin Bray, nephew of Reverend Bray.)

This image depicts Bra-Haven. Conklin—the Reverend's nephew—states on the back that, "We lived there on the corner of Virginia in 1934 and 1935. One of the things I remember most was seeing the trucks go by loaded with trees going to the paper mills in Ludington and Manistee."(Courtesy of Conklin Bray.)

Conklin Bray and wife are captured on film during their honeymoon, standing in front of Reverend and Mrs. Bray's home in Idlewild. (Courtesy of Conklin Bray.)

Bra-Haven is shown here during the winter season. (Courtesy of Conklin Bray.)

Reverend Bray pastored the church for 16 years and resigned due to failing health. Before ending his final administration, however, Reverend Bray held a conference with members of his church, where they agreed that he turn over the church to the Michigan Conference of the African Methodist Episcopal Church. Lela and Herman Wilson were active members of the Tabernacle AME Church. Mr. Wilson served on the Board of Trustees. At the time of his death in 1963, the Tabernacle AME Church was in the middle of yet another major transition, move, and renovation project. The Tabernacle has served the community for nearly 80 years, 61 of those years under nearly 10 bishops. Other religious denominations and church structures that followed the Tabernacle included Mount Olive Church of God in Christ (1929), First Baptist Church of Idlewild (1933), and the Seventh Day Adventist Church (1936).

We Are Building

A Congregation   A Bible School

People's Church of Christ
and
Idlewild Community Center

THE CHURCH WITH A GOSPEL MESSAGE

SUNDAY—10:00 A. M. Bible School
11:00 A. M. Preaching by the Minister
6:00 P. M. Christian Endeavor

WEDNESDAY—6:00 P. M. Missionary Meeting
7:00 P. M. Prayer Meeting

WELCOME

The greetings in this program are from our friends.
Remember them in 1932.

THE DESIGN ON THE FRONT: This design has a long history.
The border design and coloring is taken from a hand illuminated Life of
St. Francis written by St. Bonaventure in 1504. The original page from
which the reproduction is made is in the British Museum in London. The
symbols in the corners and the bottom may be interpreted as follows:—
Upper Left: Alpha-Mu-Omega meaning Yesterday, Today and Forever;
Upper Right: Crown and Scepter meaning The King Forever; Lower Left:
Monogram of the Virgin standing for the Virgin Birth; Center at Bottom:
The Sun meaning the Sun of Righteousness; Bottom Right: The Candle
and Candlestick meaning Jesus, the Light of the World.

CHRISTMAS PROGRAM, 1931
People's Church of Christ and Idlewild Community Center
Rev. H. Franklin Bray, D. D., Minister   Idlewild, Michigan

This is a 1931 Christmas program from the People's Church of Christ and Idlewild Community Center. (Courtesy of Susan Dooley, Yates Township Public Library.)

TABERNACLE

DAY

IN IDLEWILD

MEN'S DAY

AUGUST 3, 1952

A

SOUVENIR

PROGRAM

PRICE 75c

Another souvenir program, this time from Tabernacle Men's Day, which occurred on August 3, 1952. (Courtesy of Susan Dooley, Yates Township Public Library.)

On Sunday, August 20, 1978, the 22nd Annual Women's Day event was held by the First Baptist Church of Idlewild. (Courtesy of Susan Dooley, Yates Township Public Library.)

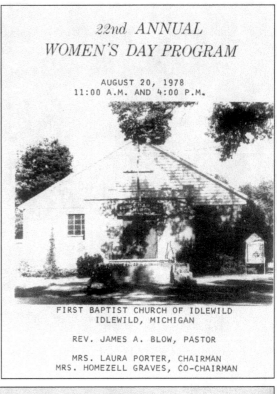

The original First Baptist Church of Idlewild building was built in 1935 on land donated by the Idlewild Resort Company. (Courtesy of Ronald J. Stephens.)

Here is an interior view of Tabernacle services. (From the private collection of Dawn Light Centre, Inc.)

THE LIFE AND TIMES
of
JOHN (JAY) CALVIN PELLUM

The cover page of the obituary, with photograph of Elder John Calvin Pellum, founder and pastor of the Mount Olive Church of God in Christ. (From the private collection of Dawn's Light Centre, Inc.)

Five

THE WILSON LEGACY

Herman O. and Lela G. Wilson came to Idlewild in 1915 as part of the first excursion from Chicago sponsored by the Idlewild Resort Company. On this visit they dreamed and determined that this was a land of opportunity with a bright future. In 1921 they moved to Idlewild and built their first home in the newly founded African American resort. Their first home was a log cabin in the woods west of Lincoln Park on Lynndon Street. Following the couple's success in selling lots in their first plat, they purchased more land ranging from the railroad tracks on the north side of Paradise Lake, and south along Forman Road to Baldwin Road. They developed the Plat of Wilson's Paradise Garden Number One and Wilson's Paradise Garden Number Two. The next two plats contained 1,747 additional lots, most of which were sold by 1932. In addition to the property in these plats, they owned vast sums of land all over Lake County including an oil well in Peacock Township. In the *Negro Digest*, August 1958 edition, it was estimated that their holdings were valued at $250,000.

The Wilson's were active in community development and local government. Mr. Wilson served as Yates Township supervisor, trustee, justice of the peace, constable and highway commissioner at various times in the early 1930s and 1940s. He also served as a trustee on the Yates Township School Board. Mrs. Wilson, fondly called "L.G." by business associates, built homes and commercial buildings throughout the area. The current Idlewild Post Office building on Essex Boulevard is one of the buildings that she built. The famous Paradise Club and the Paradise Hotel were also part of the Paradise Resort Complex. In the early 1950s, the community annually recognized Mr. and Mrs. Herman O. and Lela G. Wilson by honoring them as pioneering citizens who helped to shape the destiny of Idlewild by designating August 23 as Wilson Day. What was a nebulous dream for the Wilson's became a concrete reality — from coast to coast, Idlewild was one of America's leading resorts, and the Wilson's played a significant role in its development.

RESORT DEVELOPMENT

Having purchased a number of lots on Idlewild Lake, Mrs. Wilson became the Idlewild Resort Company's most successful saleswoman. In 1922 the Wilson's purchased the Frank Haven farm, an 80-acre parcel of land which ran east and west from Tampa Avenue to Tacoma Boulevard and north, and south from Baldwin Road to the southern shore of Paradise Lake. They subdivided this land into the first plat of Wilson's Paradise Garden. On July 10, 1922 the Yates Township Board approved this plat. The Lake County Plat Board approved this plat on September 13, 1922. Ready for sale this plat contained 12 blocks with 424 lots of various sizes around the southern shore of Paradise Lake. In the middle of this plat they developed a wide two-lane road with a median strip. The road was named Paradise Path, and it ran north and south from Baldwin Road to Wilson Road. This was the main road into the Paradise Lake Resort Complex. The Wilson's built their home from large stones collected throughout Idlewild by Lela Wilson. They also built a hotel, a clubhouse, a bed and breakfast, and several guest cottages as part of the Paradise Resort Complex.

The home of Herman O. and Lela G. Wilson on Wilson Drive in the early 1930s. The house was built from large stones collected by Lela. The Wilson's home is now owned by Mr. and Mrs. Joe and Fredna Lindsey of Islewild. (From the private collection of Maryellen Wilson.)

Their first grocery store was an attached structure in the garage at the rear of their home. Standing near the counter of the grocery store are H. O. Wilson, Sr., Bernice and John Simons, serving Mrs. Beulah Riddles, and Herman O. Wilson, Jr., with his hands on his head. The Wilson's first grocery was built in 1928 to accommodate tourism. (Courtesy of Herman O. Wilson, Jr.)

Joe Louis visited Idlewild at least on two occasions. Hugging Herman O. Wilson, Jr., Joe Louis, c. 1939, is seen kneeing down to pose on the dock of Paradise Lake. (Courtesy of Herman O. Wilson, Jr.)

The Wilson's second grocery, built in 1948, was located across the street from their home, next to the Paradise Hotel. (Courtesy of Maryellen Wilson.)

The new grocery included a gas pump to the right of the structure. Herman O. Wilson, Sr. is standing on the side of the grocery in front of the two gas pumps on Wilson Drive. (From the private collection of Maryellen Wilson.)

This is a roadside view of the Paradise Club (which was built in 1928), before it was converted to the Paradise Nightclub around 1948. (From the private collection of Maryellen Wilson.)

Roadside view of the Paradise Club, with 1950s automobiles parked in various locations around the nightclub, c. 1959. Observe the banner hanging over the entranceway, which highlights featured entertainment at the club for July 25. (Photographed and mass printed postcard by the L.L. Cook Company of Milwaukee, Courtesy of John Fraser Hart.)

Like the Wilson Grocery, the club had to have a license in order to sell liquor to customers. Although it is unclear when Mr. Wilson applied and obtained a license to sale liquor, Michigan lawmakers required all nightclubs to have a dancing license as well. This is the Paradise Club dancing and liquor license, issued to John Simmons in 1942. (Courtesy of the Idlewild Historical Museum and Cultural Center.)

The Wilson's were located on Paradise Path, a unique feature in the Paradise Resort Complex because of the two lane gravel roads leading to and from Baldwin Road to Wilson Drive with a median down the center that housed lush flower beds filled with beautiful flowers, and rich evergreen shrubs. (From the private collection of Maryellen Wilson.)

The Paradise Hotel, later known as "Heartbreak Hotel," was built in 1929. The lovely Paradise Hotel was the first hotel on Paradise Lake. It housed many of the tourists that came to Idlewild from 1929 to 1964. It also had a photography studio in the front room next to the fireplace where many of the noted visitors who toured Idlewild posed for portraits. (From the private collection of Maryellen Wilson.)

Mr. and Mrs. Herman O. Wilson, Maryellen Wilson, other Wilson relatives and close friends of the Wilsons, are seen during a Wilson Day Celebration in the Fiesta Room of the Paradise Club in 1957. Wilson Day was founded by Mrs. Anna L. Jones of Chicago in the early 1950s. (From the private collection of Maryellen Wilson.)

Lela G. Wilson and Leona Simmons on tour through Illinois, Missouri, and Oklahoma, c. 1934. (Courtesy of Herman O. Wilson, Jr.)

Lela G. Wilson, with Arthur Braggs standing behind her, at the Paradise Club during Wilson's Day in the late 1950s. (Courtesy of Herman O. Wilson, Jr.)

THE IDLEWILD GARDEN CLUB
I'VE A WONDERFUL BLOOMING GARDEN

After developing the Paradise Resort Complex and a booming real estate business, Lela Wilson was principle in the development of the Idlewild Public Library through her leading membership and organization of the Idlewild Garden Club (IGC). Annual projects of IGC, which was founded in 1943, significantly contributed to the beautification of major sites in the community. Active members regularly met and planned annually to plant evergreens at the Post Office, the Library, First Baptist Church, Mount Olive Church of God in Christ, and the Tabernacle Community Church. Flowers were also planted throughout the community at the Yates School (from the mid-1960s to the late 1970s), the Oaklawn Cemetery Entrance, and the Lot Owner's Association Youth Center. The club's motto, "As we share the joys of this companionship, we learn the meaning of true friendship. Together we stand, divided we fall. All for one and one for all," and their slogan, "Clean up—paint up—keep up," also conveyed a sense of family and community. Planning annual calendar events, including but not limited to the following, the club achieved the following projects:

INSTALLATION	*February*
ARBOR DAY	*April*
OAKLAWN CEMETERY	*May*
ANNUAL SERMON	*June*
GARDEN SHOW	*August*
CHRISTMAS PROJECT & DINNER	*December*

The Idlewild Garden Club is celebrating its 25th anniversary in this photograph. (From the private collection of Maryellen Wilson.)

Idlewild Garden Club
1969-70

This is a IGC Program Cover, c. 1969–70, with inserted poem (p. 1) and club song (p. 4). (From the private collection of Maryellen Wilson.)

In memoriam to Lela G. Wilson, the poem reads:

> She too, had a dream.
> A place to live and work.
> A place to rest or play.
> A place of peace and beauty.
> We call it Idlewild.
> She called it Paradise.

CLUB SONG:

I've a wonderful blooming garden. All planted with flowers gay. It will bloom in spring and summer. 'Neath skies that are blue or gray. In my wonderful flower garden, I've planted the seeds of love. And the blossoms are fair and fragrant. And pleasing to God above.

This flyer announces the IGC event, Fantasy of Flowers and Art Craft Show, July 26 and 27, 1974, at the Masonic Hall on Foreman Road. (From the private collection of Maryellen Wilson.)

The club published biweekly club activity reports that were documented in *The Lake County Star*. The club remained active until the mid-1980s when most of its members became elderly and no longer active in growing and planting flowers and plants. Also linked to Lela G. Wilson's desire to beautify Idlewild back then, was the fact that she considered herself a student of metaphysics. Lela's spirituality and belief in naming spaces is revealed through the designated street names in the plats of Wilson's Paradise Garden Number One and Two. In the first plat she named the streets after cities and towns. In the next two plats she named the streets Unity, Patience, Kindness, Sincerity, Generosity, Harmony, Sunset, Wisdom, Righteous Road, Grandeur, Miracle, Creation, Justice, Perfection, and Joy.

IDLEWILD GARDEN CLUB

PRESENTS

FANTASY OF FLOWER AND ART CRAFT SHOW

July 26 and 27, 1974

FRIDAY -- 1:00 P.M. TO 5 P.M.
SATURDAY - 11:00 A.M. TO 4 P.M.

Masonic Hall on Forman Road - Idlewild

PRIZES AWARDED - 3:00 P.M. - JULY 27, 1974

President - Muriel Castallante

Seen here is the Idlewild Post Office, built by Lela G. Wilson. (From the private collection of Maryellen Wilson.)

A sky view of Wilson's Grocery, Paradise Hotel, Paradise Club, and Paradise Lake. (From the private collection of Maryellen Wilson.)

This is a photograph of Mr. Mrs. Herman O. Wilson. (From the private collection of Herman O. Wilson.)

Six

THE UNIA, DEPRESSION YEARS, AND CCC CAMP NUMBER 1691

When African-American soldiers returned home at the end of World War I, they only found the status quo. Leading black leaders such as Dr. Du Bois protested strenuously against this blatant inequity of African-American soldiers fighting a war to preserve human rights and democracy on a foreign shore while being denied these same rights to them on U.S. soil. Regarding the plight of African Americans as unsalvageable under white rule, Idlewilders were attracted to the philosophy of the Honorable Marcus Mosiah Garvey and the Universal Negro Improvement Association and African Communities League (UNIA-ACL). Michigan had 14 divisions of the UNIA-ACL, including one in Idlewild, and a chapter in Detroit. Garvey's thundering voice motivated Idlewild residents to take pride in their community and culture. Although Garvey's UNIA-ACL movement began to fragment and decline by the late 1920s, Garvey was successful in encouraging one faction of the population in Idlewild to continue to establish their own commercial enterprises.

In 1927, John H. and Ella J. Hawthorne purchased five lots of property in Paradise Gardens from Lela Wilson and donated the property to Division No. 895, (later to become Division No. 126) UNIA-ACL of Idlewild. Liberty Hall, as these meeting sites were called, was built by December 1928 on Baldwin Road near Tampa Avenue. It was used for various community activities, spanning the years 1929 to the late 1960s.

After serving two years and nine months in prison, the Honorable Marcus Mosiah Garvey was pardoned by President Calvin Coolidge and immediately deported to Jamaica. On board the SS *Saramacca* before his deportation from New Orleans to Jamaica in 1927, Marcus Garvey (3rd from left) poses with a group of UNIA officials: (left to right) Joseph A. Craigen, executive secretary, Detroit division; S.V. Robertson, president, Cleveland division; Garvey; E.B. Knox, Garvey's personal representative; William Ware (rear, almost hidden), president, Cincinnati division; and Dr. J.J. Peters, president, New Orleans division. (From the Marcus Garvey Papers, in the New York Public Library, Schomburg Center for Research in Black Culture.)

UNIA, Division No. 895 was renumbered in 1930 as Division No. 126, Liberty Hall. The building was torn down during the Idlewild Renewal Initiative of 1974-75. (From the private collection of Dawn's Light Centre, Inc.)

Mrs. Vina Galloway Smith, Lady President, and her sister, Elizabeth Thompson from Chicago are shown above. Adam Daniel Smith, Vina's husband, is not shown. However, he served as the division's reporter for its first five years. (From the private collection of Katherine Smith-Kendall.)

Pictured is the Idlewild Community Hall where Marcus Garvey supposedly spoke in 1929, after secretly traveling to Idlewild. While it's not clear when or if Garvey ever traveled to Idlewild or in whose home he stayed while there, several senior citizens claim they remember seeing him and hearing him speak. Garvey was deported in 1927. (From the private collection of Iris J. Hill.)

CIVILIAN CONSERVATION CORPS, CAMP BALDWIN, CAMP NO. 1691

During the Great Depression, President Franklin Delano Roosevelt called the 73rd Congress into emergency session on March 31, 1933, and issued an Emergency Conservation Works Act, which became known as the Civilian Conservation Corps (CCC). Roosevelt's CCC Program enrolled thousands of 18- to 25-year-old unmarried men in a peacetime army setting. The goal of the program was to have them engage in a battle against mounting destruction of our natural resources. Michigan's Manistee National Forest was used to secure employment opportunities for economically disadvantaged youth. Approximately 167 African-American men from Detroit metropolitan and rural areas were inducted into an All-Colored CCC Camp in western Michigan. Located on Nelson Road in Yates Township, the men of Camp Baldwin fought forest fires, improved and reclaimed millions of acres from soil erosion, and developed Michigan roads and trails covering an area of 59,000 acres, most of which was owned by the state. When not working, the men regularly attended Tabernacle worship services, the Purple Palace Club, and UNIA dinner dances in Idlewild. They also participated in such sports as swimming, boxing, track, and baseball.

The exterior of barracks for Civilian Conservation Corp, Camp Baldwin, Camp No. 1691. (From the private collection of Salona Cleveland Brown.)

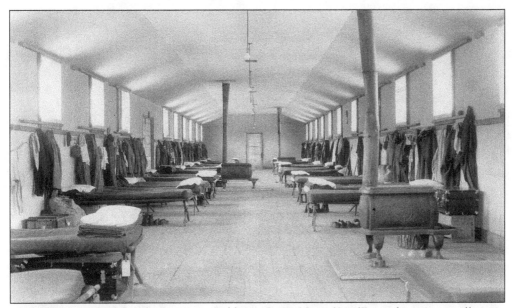

The interior of the barracks for Camp Baldwin, Camp No. 1691. (From the private collection of Salona Cleveland Brown.)

Pictured is the Camp Baldwin, Camp No.1691 Baseball Team. The names of the baseball team from bottom row, left to right: Roosevelt Fulwood, Doctor Holiday, and Eddie Tucker; (second from bottom row) Olie Lewis, Oscar Carrothers, Mr. Blake, Dan Ouden, Jack Drayton, Hank Beard; third row: Charlie, Charlie Bassie, Robert Bagley, Sandford Jackson, Smitty (the cook), and Jackson; (fourth row, top) Shorty Grear, Zazu Pitts, unidentified, and Burt McCarn. (From the private collection of Salona Cleveland Brown.)

The men of Camp No. 1691, Camp Baldwin, are shown. (From the private collection of Salona Cleveland Brown.)

This is the historic marker memorializing the site of the Civilian Conservation Corp, Camp Baldwin, Camp No.1691, 1933–1942, c. October 1994. Standing behind the marker is Norman Burns, Yates Township Supervisor, 1992–2000. Also present is Leonard Wyatt, standing to the far right, who was one of the original CCC men. (Courtesy of Ronald J. Stephens.)

Seven

THE HEYDAY
ENTERTAINMENT ERA

During the post-World War II era a renewed interest in Idlewild unfolded. New African-American entrepreneurs, taking advantage of the community's commercial potential, purchased and managed property on Williams Island and Paradise Gardens, and developed classy shows in two nightspots. The names Phil Giles, who owned the Flamingo Club and Giles Hotel, and Arthur Braggs, who leased and managed the Paradise Club, became synonymous with Idlewild. From 1952 to 1964, featured entertainers in both clubs included Della Reese, Al Hibbler, Bill Doggertt, Jackie Wilson, T-Bone Walker, The Four Tops, George Kirby, Roy Hamilton, Brooks Benton, and Choker Campbell.

PHIL GILES ENTERPRISES

Phil Giles came to Idlewild in 1948, and opened a riding stable on Williams Island next to the old Purple Palace Nightclub. A bar with an outdoor garden was built in 1949, known as the Flamingo Bar. It was noted for its décor of flamingo pink with pictures of flamingos painted on all of the walls, and large mirrors with flamingos on them. This was the beginning of the Phil Giles Enterprises, which included the purchase of the Oakmere Hotel on Williams Island, remodeled and renamed the Hotel Giles. In 1955, a 500-seat nightclub was added onto the bar.

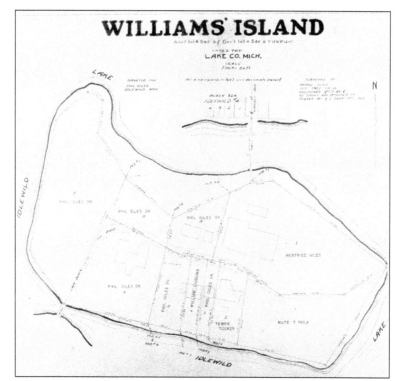

Plat of the Phil Giles Enterprise on Williams Island. (Courtesy of the Idlewild Historical Museum and Cultural Center.)

Phil Giles Dude Ranch was built in 1948 on the Island, and was the first building constructed by Phil Giles Enterprises. Standing in front of the building from left to right are Charles Coykendall, Bea Giles, and Phil Giles. (From the private collection of "Mama" Helen Curry.)

Phil Giles Flamingo Bar. The Phil Giles Flamingo Bar was built in 1949 on William's Island. Delightful and congenial surroundings located directly across from beautiful Lake Idlewild. The Flamingo Bar, featuring television, dancing, and five beverages for your vacation pleasure, was opened from May 1 to December 1. (From the private collection of Dawn's Light Centre, Inc.)

This is the interior of the Flamingo Club dining room. (From the private collection of Dawn's Light Centre, Inc.)

This brochure, *Come to Beautiful Idlewild for a Real Vacation*, was issued by the Idlewild Chamber of Commerce. (Courtesy of Ronald J. Stephens.)

Portrait of Phil Giles, owner of the Phil Giles Enterprise. (Courtesy of Betty Foote.)

"Mama" Helen Curry working the bar at the Flamingo Club. (From the private collection of Mama Helen.)

Trixie Aldrich worked as an exotic dancer, talent agent, and entertainment coordinator for Phil and Bea Giles. Trixie is seen working behind the bar at the Flamingo Club. (Courtesy of Dottie Rose.)

Phil Giles is credited with promoting entertainment in Idlewild (including the shows produced by Braggs) as America's most famous resort. In addition to the shows, Phil Giles built many buildings on Williams Island that promoted the resort area. The Grill was noted for its 26-cent hamburgers in the early 1950s. There was a barbecue stand, shrimp hut, and a boat ride concession stand he established on the lake that attracted thousands of tourists to the community. He dubbed Idlewild as "The Resort Capital of America." And while Braggs attracted classy up and coming local, regional, national and international acts, Phil Giles' Flamingo Club offered more local and regional entertainment for Idlewilders. He also offered the latest sounds and good food, drink, and interpersonal interactions. Both Phil Giles and Arthur Braggs put Idlewild on the map. Giles invested heavily into the community, while Braggs invested in the shows and the performers. Giles owned a hotel and restaurants that he developed and sold to other black entrepreneurs. So many people came to Idlewild on weekends and holidays that the state of Michigan sent National Guard details to help with traffic control. In 1951, the community established its own police department, and *Jet Magazine* published an article about Officer Patricia Hoskins in 1955, recognizing her as the first African-American mounted policewoman in the United States. Phil Giles pioneered the nightclub era in the 1950s, making Idlewild one of the most famous African-American resorts in the United States.

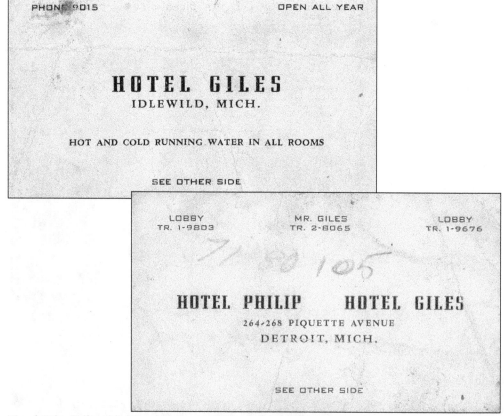

Hotel Giles (Idlewild), Hotel Philip, and Hotel Giles (Detroit), are shown on both sides of this business card (Courtesy of Geraldine Hamilton Wooley).

This photograph captures Luther Thompson and the Flamingo Dancers during a performance. (Phil Giles' Theatrical Agency, Courtesy of Cliniece Stubbs.)

A shake dancer doing the split while performing in the Flamingo Club. She was known as "Black Velvet" and was a very popular exotic dancer at the Paradise and Flamingo Clubs. This picture was taken when she was appearing with B.B. King at Roberts Show Lounge on the South Side of Chicago, c. 1959. (Courtesy of Mama Helen Curry.)

Dottie Rose and Squeakie standing in front of the Phil Giles Flamingo Bar and Club, one of Michigan's largest and most fabulous entertainment centers. Featuring ALL STAR bands and entertainers, the complete establishment was built in the early 1950s and opened in 1955. (Courtesy of Dottie Rose.)

Dottie Rose Style Show at the Flamingo Club in 1967. Everyone who participated wore paper cloth. Hers was a paper pantsuit and hat. (Courtesy of Dottie Rose.)

This photograph shows the Phil Giles Hotel. (From the private collection of Dawn's Light Centre.)

Mr. Giles was a member of various organizations, including the Idlewild Lot Owners' Association, the Detroit Idlewilders, president of the Idlewild African-American Chamber of Commerce, and he became the first African American to belong to the Baldwin Rotary Club. Mr. Giles was also elected Yates Township Supervisor in 1951, serving the community in that capacity until 1959. He, along with Lela Wilson, traveled around the nation making Idlewild known to all that would listen. He attracted many tourists to invest in the community and was instrumental in stimulating the economy until the recession of 1958, which caused a severe economic disaster in the state of Michigan. Mr. Giles was the mayor of Idlewild. He, Dr. Daniel Hale Williams, Lela G. Wilson, and Arthur "Daddy" Braggs were the leading entrepreneurs of the 1920s, 1930s, 1940s and 1950s.

Shake dancers performing
at the Flamingo Club.
(Courtesy of Tommy Roy.)

Original Chicago Idlewilders' Line Dancing on the dance floor at the Flamingo Club. (From
the private collection of Maryellen Wilson.)

74

Original Chicago Idlewilders', including Gladys Chipchase (second from left) and E. Ann Hawkins (far right) at Club El Morocco. (Courtesy of Dottie Rose.)

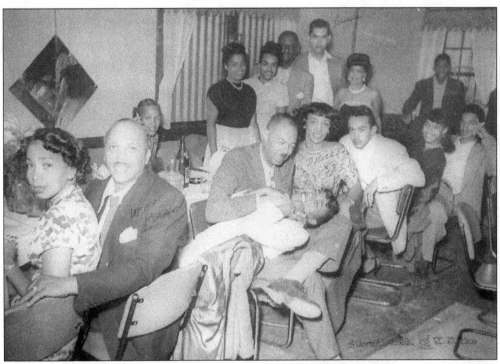

When the evening ended in the Flamingo and Paradise Nightclubs, the crowds headed for Club El Morocco, the after-hours spot that was built in 1924 by Jovana De Hajara. (Courtesy of Dottie Rose.)

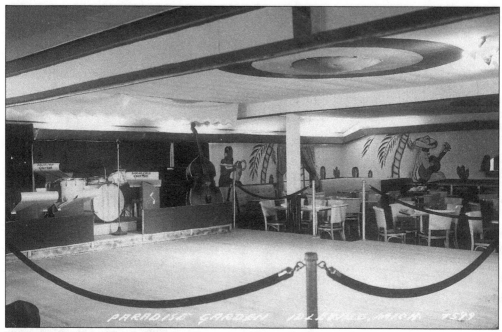

The interior of the Paradise Club. (Courtesy of Francelle Morrow.)

One of the dancers would spray paint his entire body with some sort of gold paint to look like—are you ready for this?—Hollywood Oscar. Some Idlewilders remember heeing him eating fire, too. (Courtesy of Tommy Roy.)

This is an inside view of the Paradise Club with Arthur "Daddy" Braggs. Seated from left to right are Sarah Vaugn, Arthur Braggs, his wife Leodell, and Choker Campbell. (From the private collection of Carlean Gill.)

ARTHUR BRAGGS, THE PARADISE NIGHTCLUB, AND THE IDLEWILD REVUE

When Arthur Braggs, a Saginaw businessman who owned the Hickory House, managed the Paradise Nightclub, Idlewild was on the verge of becoming a major entertainment center. Over the course of the next decade, Braggs was determined to recruit and attract many famous and electrifying talents to Idlewild, including Bill Doggett, Della Reese, Al Hibbler, Sarah Vaughan, Jackie Wilson. T-Bone Walker, George Kirby, the Dyerettes, Roy Hamilton, Brooks Benton, Choker Campbell, Little Willie John, Dakota Station, the Rhythm Kings, the Harlem Brothers, and the fabulous Four Tops. Braggs had a dream to build the Summer Apollo of Michigan, a vision that was far ahead of its time. Braggs invested heavily in the shows he produced in the Fiesta Room at the Paradise Club, and in cities throughout the United States and Montreal, Canada. He understood that patrons of his nightclub and the clubs his shows toured could not go elsewhere, so he created a classy atmosphere that was far better than shows anywhere in the world. At the Paradise Club, Joe "Ziggy" Johnson was the Master of Ceremony, and Pinkney Roberts performed that role in his absence. These men were top-notch and so too were shows that they were to emcee throughout the 1950s and early 1960s. The shows were classy and first-rate, featuring bright lights, quality sounds, large crowds, excellent food and service, and classy costumes worn by the showgirls. These costumes were not only colorful and glittering, but they were designed by leading designers from Chicago and New York. They were as good as any you would see in Las Vegas. These shows were simply glamorous.

During all of the shows, the job of the show girls was to look beautiful, while the dancers and other acts were simply talented. The chorus girls danced in high heel shoes. When it was time to "Bury the show" in Idlewild, the day after Labor Day, one of the final treats for their audience, in addition to some great movement and vocal performances, was when the singers would become the dancers and the dancers would become the singers. Arthur Braggs' Idlewild Revue toured the United States and Canada where they performed in Detroit at the Flame Show Bar and Zombies in Paradise Valley, in Chicago at Robert's Show Lounge, the Tivoli Theater, and Club Delisa; at the Apollo Theater and Wilt Chamberlain's Small Paradise Café in Harlem; at The Orchid Room in Kansas City, Missouri; The Pink Poodle in Indianapolis; the Vagabond Room in Cleveland, OH, and other venues in Boston, Washington, D.C., Baltimore, Philadelphia, Buffalo, Kansas City, Kansas, and Oklahoma; as well as the Black Orchid in the Canadian metropolitan areas of Montreal, Toronto and Quebec City. They performed at many of the popular nightspots in those cities. Braggs along with Ziggy Johnson directed Arthur Braggs Idlewild Revue, while Tommy Roy, a popular radio personality for WKLA in Ludington, handled publicity, promotion, and public relations.

Promotional shot of Della Reese, who performed at the Paradise Club before going professional in the early 1950s and appearing on the Ed Sullivan Show. By the middle-1950s, Della Reese had more records on the market, and was one of the only artists besides Al Hibbler who could readily sell records in three market fields: jazz, pop, and blues. (Exclusive RCA Victor Recording Artist from the private collection of Mr. Tommy Roy.)

Bill Doggett cut one of the biggest hits of all-time in 1956 when his two-part song, *Honky Tonk*, hit the air waves. This is a promotional shot of Doggett, who performed for five consecutive years in Idlewild; four at the Paradise Club, and one at the Flamingo Nightclub, before and after the song became a hit. (From the private collection of Tommy Roy.)

The Rhythm Kings of Chicago were a big hit in Idlewild and on tour with the Arthur Braggs Idlewild Revue. Left to right are performers Kenny Mitchell, Sonny Montgomery, and Bobby Murphy. (From the private collection of Minnie Murphy.)

Promotional shot of Pinkney Roberts, who served as the master of ceremonies for many of the shows at the Paradise Club. (Courtesy of Tommy Roy.)

Jackie Wilson, the entertainer's entertainer, was something on and off stage. Known as Mr. Excitement, Jackie Leroy Wilson would literally charm the ladies while on stage. Susan Morse, a *Detroit Free Press* writer, states, "He was dubbed for the writhing, microphone-tossing, energy-charged performances that moved young audiences to a frenzy." With classic songs like "Lonely Teardrops" and "Doggin' Around," Jackie Wilson became a symbol. Kneeing down the front entrance of the Paradise Club, where he performed regularly, Jackie and others pose for the camera shirtless. It must have been a hot summer afternoon. (From the private collection of Carlean Gill.)

The Four Tops got their start in Idlewild while performing at the Paradise Club and on tour with The Arthur Braggs' Idlewild Revue. From left to right: Lawrence Payton, Renaldo "Obie" Benson, Levi Stubbs, Jr., and Abdul "Duke" Fakir. In those days, the group performed with one microphone. Stubbs, Fakir, and Benson have been together for over 36 years, constantly producing songs of love, happiness and romantic heartbreak in the tradition of the Detroit "Motown" Sound. Besides producing repeated hits on the top ten list like "Baby I Need Your Loving," "I Can't Help Myself, and Reach Out" to their credit, no other popular quartet has stayed together with its original personnel for as long as the legendary Four Tops. (Courtesy of Cliniece Stubbs.)

The Harlem Brothers of Chicago also performed at the Paradise Club. From left to right are Duke, Kip, and Rico. (Courtesy of Donna Dixion-Harvey.)

Here are a couple of show girls on stage at the Paradise Club, from one of the many production numbers which were always so popular in the Idlewild Revue. (From the private collection of Carlean Gill.)

Here are the members of the Arthur Braggs' 1960 Idlewild Revue. From left to right are the following: (clockwise, beginning at bottom left) Norma Washington, Val Benson, Carlean Gill, Ricky Ford, Cliniece Stubbs, unknown, and Inez Fakir (two in center, from left to right) Roger Bryant Fluker, and George Patterson. (From the private collection of Carlean Gill.)

Pictured are the Dyerettes, from left to right: Gloria Broussard Wilkes, Clarice White Pruitt, Shirley Hall Bass, Muriel Wilson Foster, and Vera Wilson Mann.

This is a promotional shot of comedian, impressionist, singer, dancer, and actor George Kirby. This man could do it all. He was also the opening act for some of the greatest names in show business. George toured with the Arthur Braggs' Idlewild Revue, telling many jokes while experiencing racism on the road. He was also the performer who popularized Arthur Braggs' as "Daddy" Braggs. (Courtesy of Arnell Pugh.)

Lottie "The Body" Tatum-Graves performed at the Paradise Club and on tour with Arthur Braggs' Idlewild Revue. Lottie was a very popular exotic dancer in Idlewild, Detroit, and throughout the United States. (Courtesy of Lottie "The Body" Tatum-Graves.)

This is a promotional shot of Ruth Brown who also performed at the Paradise Club. (Courtesy of Tommy Roy.)

83

Upper left: Shown here is Arthur Prysock. (Courtesy of Arnell Pugh.)

Upper Right: Lon Fontaine was a very popular dancer and choreographer in Idlewild at the Paradise Club. He also toured with The Arthur Braggs' Idlewild Revue and The Larry Steele Smart Affairs Revue of Chicago and Atlantic City, New Jersey. (Courtesy of Arnell Pugh.)

Bottom Left: Brooks Benton, a chart topper, also performed at Idlewild. (Courtesy of Arnell Pugh.)

This is an inside view of the Paradise Club with Arthur "Daddy" Braggs. Seating from left to right are Arthur Braggs, his wife, Leodell "Tudelum", unknown woman, Robert "Buddy" Rose, and unknown man. (From the private collection of Carlean Gill.)

Louie Jordan and the Tymphony Five showcased their talents at Idlewild. (Courtesy of Arnell Pugh.)

Upper Left: Carlean Gill, Joe "Ziggy" Johnson, and Ricky Ford taking a moment to pose while at the Flame Show Bar in Detroit. (From the private collection of Carlean Gill.)

Upper Right: Julian Swain poses with the Fiesta Dolls (with Ricky Ford to his right) at the Paradise Club in the Fiesta Room. (From the private collection of Dick Mask.)

Bottom Left: Promotional shot of Betty "Bebop" Carter. (Courtesy of Tommy Roy.)

Dick Mask, Paradise Club waiter, cruises down Wilson Drive in a 1956 Cadillac convertible, sporting Paradise Club show girls. (From the private collection of Dottie Rose.)

Promotional flyer of Arthur Braggs' 1960 Idlewild Revue featuring Earl Grant, the Four Tops, the Rhythm Kings, the Fiesta Dolls, and the Braggettes at the Orchid Room in Kansas City, Missouri.

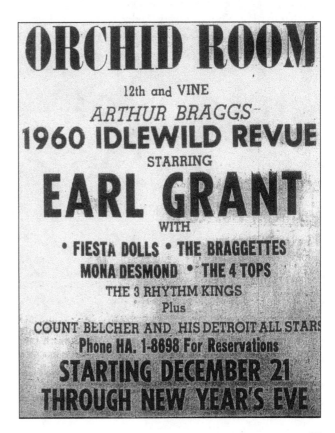

ORCHID ROOM

12th and VINE

ARTHUR BRAGGS

1960 IDLEWILD REVUE

STARRING

EARL GRANT

WITH

• FIESTA DOLLS • THE BRAGGETTES
MONA DESMOND • THE 4 TOPS
THE 3 RHYTHM KINGS
Plus

COUNT BELCHER AND HIS DETROIT ALL STARS

Phone HA. 1-8698 For Reservations

STARTING DECEMBER 21
THROUGH NEW YEAR'S EVE

Braggs conveyed a love for children in the community. Sunday afternoons there was a matinee for young people, who would have dinner and see great entertainment. Out of this experience some children even performed and became great entertainers themselves. In this image, Carlean Gill and her nieces and nephew are at a Sunday matinee at the Paradise Club on August 11, 1962. Observe the knockers on the tables in front of everyone seated at the table from left to right. Knockers were used to signify fan pleasure following a performance. Seated are Norman, Winita, Rosa, Bonnie, and Carlean. (From the private collection of Carlean Gill.)

Scouting for performers, Braggs took trips to Mexico. He met the Leon Escobar Dancers on one of these trips. One of the dancers with the Leon Escobar Dancers was a Mexican dancer known as Aida Casablanc. They were extremely popular with the Idlewild crowd. Staging some enormous production numbers, Braggs was convinced he needed to recruit the group and especially Aida from Mexico as a featured act that toured with the Idlewild Revue. (From the private collection of Carlean Gill.)

Carlean Gill modeling at the
Paradise Club Fiesta Room. Carlean
Gill was one of Braggs Fiesta Dolls.
The Fiesta Dolls (Jo Ella, Betty
Joe, Carlean, Mickey, and Ricky
Ford), whose main job was to look
good, didn't sweat as much as
the Braggetts. (From the private
collection of Carlean Gill.)

The original Ziggy Johnson Dancers at Club Zombie in Detroit. From left to right, they are Donna
Dixion-Harvey, Valiada Talley-Benson, Cliniece Townsend-Stubbs, and Inez Clinscables-Fakir.
Before becoming the Braggetts with the Arthur Braggs Idlewild Revue, they were teenage dancers
known as the Ziggy Johnson Dancers in Detroit. (Courtesy of Cliniece Stubbs.)

Carlean Gill, unknown, Ricky Ford, and unknown pose standing in Idlewild Lake near the beach on Williams Island. (From the private collection of Carlean Gill.)

Promotional flyer of the Arthur Braggs' 1963 Idlewild Revue at the Vagabond Room in Cleveland, Ohio. (From the private collection of Carlean Gill.)

The Idlewild Revue. From left to right, Otis Stanley, Clineice Stubbs, Carlean Gill, Unknown, Mickey Roberts, Pinkney Roberts, Betty Jo Cave, Val Benson, Jo Ella Keough, unknown, and Roger Bryan Fluker. (From the private collection of Carlean Gill.)

Promotional flyer of the Arthur Braggs' 1962 Idlewild Revue at the Black Orchid Casino in the heart of Montreal, Canada. (From the private collection of Carlean Gill.)

This is the Black Orchid Casino, located in Montreal, Canada. (From the private collection of Carlean Gill.)

A photograph of Cuban Pete in the Paradise Club with Herman Cedric Collins. (Courtesy of Arnell Pugh.)

Arnell Pugh was one of the
show girls and dancers for the
Arthur Braggs' Idlewild Revue.
(Courtesy of Arnell Pugh.)

Cast children on stage at the Paradise
Club during one of the Sunday matinee.
Herman Cedric Collins to the left with
Bruce Glenn in striped shirt to the right
doing the twist in the summer of 1962.
(Courtesy of Arnell Pugh.)

Arthur Braggs' Paradise Club closed down in the mid-1960s. Braggs returned to Saginaw, Michigan continuing his business endeavors. While Braggs enjoyed a successful business career, in 1966 the economy in Idlewild began to decline. Braggs appeared subsequently on a PBS Special, *Summer of '58*, with Della Reese, Jackie Wilson, and George Kirby in the early 1970s.

Braggs loved horses, attended the tracks, and consequently invested in the horse racing business. Carlean Gill and Arthur Braggs can be seen standing in front of Jockey Timothy Kelly on Ron Roman at the Charles Town Race Track in West Virginia. (From the private collection of Carlean Gill.)

Braggs established a personal relationship with many of the male employees and performers of the Paradise Club in Idlewild. Seated is Braggs, standing to his right is Goose Tatum, and above is Duke Fakir, and third from the left is Dick Mask. (Courtesy of Dick Mask.)

Eight

NATIONAL
IDLEWILDER'S CLUB, INC.

In the summer of 1952, a group of long time friends from Chicago, Cleveland, Detroit, Indianapolis, and St. Louis met in Chicago to celebrate their love and friendships. The friends, who had been frequent summer vacationers in Idlewild, met and discussed ideas to organize a social club consisting of people who made Idlewild their vacation spot. By the end of the fall, friends from Chicago and Detroit respectively organized Idlewilder's chapters in their cities. In Chicago, they called themselves, the Original Chicago Idlewilders, and later split up and established a second Chicago group, called The Chicago, Inc. In Detroit they called themselves, the Detroit Idlewilder Club, Inc. Mr. Sunnie Wilson, one of the original summer visitors that met in Chicago, called a few of his Detroit friends to meet him at his Mark Twain Hotel. The idea was conceived and the founders of the Detroit chapter, which consisted of Attorney Joseph Craigen, Joseph and Velma Branam, Clarence Brown, Winola Burch-Conway, Judge Lucile Alexander-Watts and Isola Graham-Winburn, formulated concrete plans for a club. The purpose they established at both Detroit and Chicago meetings was to create an organization that would support charitable and civic endeavors and that would promote social entertainment and recreation. Six chapters, 45 years later, now comprise a national body, known as the National Idlewilder's Club, Inc. Chapters consist of the Original Chicago, the Chicago, Inc., Cleveland Wildcats, the Detroit, Mid-Michigan, and St. Louis Idlewilders.

From May to October each year, the population size in Idlewild increases from approximately 784 permanent residents to over 5,000 seasonal visitors and property owners. The main reason for this sudden increase has to do with the National Idlewilders, their participation in annual community celebrations, and their visibility in the community during Idlewilders Week in August. During Idlewilder's Week, which begins the second week of August each year, they begin with a national kick off party, followed by celebrations held by each chapter each day thereafter. Each chapter is responsible for sponsoring a full day of social activities with food and drinks for the entire organization. Club activities range from grilled breakfasts, annual cook outs, and evening parties for club members and their guests. Club members are welcomed to invite up to six guests. Events are usually held at the Detroit Idlewilders Clubhouse, the Idlewild Lot Owners' Association Clubhouse, and Morton's Motel. The National Idlewilders Club, like the National Idlewild Lot Owners Association, is a national organization, which has a national president and executive secretary. A list of national presidents include: Ocie Drake (1978–82), Riley Harper (1982–86), Luke Isler (1986–90), Willis Alexander Jackson (1991–93), E. Ann Hawkins (1994–99), and Luke Isler (1999–present).

Selected members of the National Idlewilders are also members of the ILOA. Events celebrated during Idlewilders Week include an amateur show and Fashion Flair sponsored by ILOA and supported by both clubs. In addition to these two events, the Idlewilders pay homage to their elder members with a 50s-Plus Celebration in honor of those 50 years old and older. Other subgroup activities include the Rat Pack and the Wolf Pack, which each consist of senior male club members from all chapters, and the Posses, younger male and female club members from all chapters, who promote activities to maintain group cohesiveness. Most memorable about these activities and celebrations is the camaraderie, which helps to preserve and maintain family and community traditions in Idlewild. To sustain these memories of the past and present year round and during the summer months, National Idlewilders annually celebrate organizational traditions by: (1) supporting the local chapters they belong to even if they are non-active members through membership dues; (2) promoting Idlewilders Week on a continued basis; and (3) participating in social activities year-round in their respective communities and in the cities and communities of other chapters through annual conclaves to raise the capital and to maintain contacts with friends until seeing them again during the summer months in Idlewild.

I have made friendships since I was a little girl that I still maintain. People came to Idlewild from all parts of the country. From New York to California I made those kinds of friendships, which I still maintain, across the country. I think this led into the Idlewilders club because of the love and friendships. I think it's been one of the main stays of Idlewild, and I know that my children now have friends all over the country that they still correspond with or see and all. Idlewild just means friendship when you think about it. It's very strange. I don't know of any other place that I've ever been that has been so prominent.

E. Ann Hawkins, former National President, National Idlewilders' Club, Inc.

Friendship celebration of Idlewilders in the basement of Ms. Maryellen Wilson, c. 1958. From the private collection of Maryellen Wilson, an Original Chicago Idlewilder.

Famous Comedian George Kirby was known for celebrating with Idlewilders. He's having fun during a party in the basement of Ms. Maryellen Wilson with Original Chicago Idlewilders. (From the private collection of Maryellen Wilson.)

Maryellen Wilson, George Kirby, Maw and Paw Longhorn, and other Original Chicago Idlewilders in Maryellen Wilson's basement. (From the private collection of Maryellen Wilson.)

Idlewilders rehearsing traditional line dance with Paw Longhorn leading and Maryellen Wilson far left. (From the private collection of Maryellen Wilson.)

Maryellen Wilson (left) and other Idlewilders practicing line dance steps at the Flamingo Club. (From the private collection of Maryellen Wilson.)

Idlewilders celebrating at a western-themed party at Morton's Motel in 1956. From left to right are Dottie Rose, Kenneth Mitchell, one of the three Rhythm King dancers, Elsie Perkins, and Arlene Jordan, a Paradise Club dancer.(Courtesy of Dottie Rose.)

Idlewilders performing ritual line dances outside the Detroit Idlewilders' Clubhouse during one of the annual Idlewilders' week celebrations. This photograph was taken in the early 1990s. (Courtesy of Ronald J. Stephens.)

Annual Idlewilders' Ho-Down Dinner Dance, *c.* 1993, including Detroit Idlewilder, Shirley Jewels, Detroiter Carlean Roundtree (center) and Laura Smith, another Detroit Idlewilder. (Courtesy of Shirley Jewels.)

A 1965 front page of the *Chicago Daily News*, featuring an article on the Amateur Show at the Flamingo Lounge. (Courtesy of Gladys Chipchase.)

Three of the founding members of the Detroit Idlewilders' Club, Isola Graham-Winburn, Sunnie Wilson, and Winola Conway, are shown here during a Detroit Idlewilders' Club dinner dance. (Courtesy of Isola Graham-Winburn.)

Idlewilders celebrating in the Lot Owners' Association clubhouse, during an annual Fashion Flair event. (Courtesy of Denise Bellamy).

Lady in shake suit, K.D. Flash of Idlewild, *Idlewilder's Magazine*.

This is Sunnie Wilson on the cover of *Idlewilder's Magazine*.

Seasonal Idlewilders create a unique aesthetic in their summer homes. Check out the interior of Maryellen Wilson's boathouse. (Courtesy of Denise Bellamy.)

Nine

YEAR ROUND COMMUNITY LIFE

With the advent of new retirees moving to the community a new sense of direction was fostered. In 1973, for instance, the Yates Township Board passed new ordinances and codes that prohibited the building or maintaining of unsafe structures, blight and trash, junk cars, and other areas of concern to Idlewild citizens. A planning commission, zoning board, and other policy-driven groups offered solutions for the betterment of the community. Federal Community Development Block Grants were applied for and obtained. A comprehensive Master Plan for the community was developed and many planners and consultants stepped forward to help the community to achieve funding for new senior citizen low-income housing and repairs. In 1977, under the leadership of Supervisor Harry Solomon, there was a complete makeover of the Island including naming it after Dr. Daniel Hale Williams. Funding was obtained for demolition and roadwork and the community focused on attracting middle aged, mid-career residents who could begin second careers. A public transportation system was established through Lake County in 1975. However, when the Lake County Board of Commissioners no longer wanted to support this service it was turned over to Yates' Township in 1976.

The community spent time, energy, and money on new and positive media coverage. The Idlewild Festival was established. New leaders replaced old ones. The community was praised for being "a place where people could work with a consensus." The community received support from many political leaders, both Democrat and Republican, at the state and federal level. Political, religious, civic leaders, and ordinary citizens all joined in creating a pleasant community that would provide a safe environment. With so many seasonal homes being upgraded, crime began to increase and the Yates Township Citizens Crime Patrol was organized in 1966. The new citizens moving into the community upgraded this patrol in 1978 by buying a vehicle and radios to be used by patrollers.

GOVERNMENT

Harry Solomon was Yates Township Supervisor from 1974–78. He is seen here seated at his desk in the Yates Township Office. Forty years after the death of Dr. Williams, the Solomon Administration honored Dr. Dan's many achievements by naming the island in his honor in 1977. (Courtesy of William Smith.)

BUSINESS

Leona B. Simmons was a prominent member of the community, shown here standing in her store, Lee Jon's Novelty Shop. She was the first African American to work in the Lake County Courthouse. She was appointed Deputy County Treasurer in 1935. Later she started her own business and served as Yates Township Treasurer for many years before retiring in 1984. In addition to her business and political activities, she was the organist for the Tabernacle AME Church and a writer for the *Lake County Star* for many years. John and Leona Simmons came to Idlewild in the late 1920s. They managed the Paradise Club and owned their own business. Jon was a local contractor and built many of the early cottages during the 1930s. (From the private collection of Mama Helen Curry.)

Lee Jon's Gift and Soda Bar was a popular novelty spot for seasonal and year round residents for many years. However, by the early 1980s, Mrs. Simmons collected light and phone bills, and chatted with customers before permanently closing. This gift shop operated year-round and served as a place to relax and enjoy the beauty of Idlewild. (From the private collection of Dawn's Light Centre, Inc.)

In 1949 the new Rosanna Tavern was built by Lottie Roxborough and son, Charles A. Roxborough, III. Mrs. Lottie G. Roxborough had purchased the Old Rosanna Tavern in the late 1920s from Rose Warner who originated the Rosanna Tea Room early in the 1920s. A popular standing room only bar, it was a favorite for celebrities, politicians, hunters, and the local population, who all shared the joy of being in Idlewild. The business served as a year-round community gathering spot for the volunteer firemen and other cross sections of the community. The tavern was sold to Herman McKinney and Alphonse Noll in the 1970s. In 1986 it became the B & S Bar, owned by James N. and Sharon A. Davis of Ypsilanti, Michigan. It was managed by Freddie Warren, who, with the help of Yates Township, and local friends, built a kitchen. This made the bar a greater attraction to the community. In the early 1990s, the Rosanna was purchased, renovated, and renamed the Red Rooster. Mr. and Mrs. William McClure, Jr. are the present owners. (From the private collection of Dawn's Light Centre.)

Standing inside the Rosanna Tavern behind the bar are Charles Anthony Roxborough III (a.k.a. Sunny Roxborough) and Audrey Kathryn Bullett in July 1965. (From the private collection of Dawn's Light Centre.)

The Casa Blanca Hotel was once owned by W. C. Coombs, who came to Idlewild in 1945 and built the hotel. The Casa Blanca, which opened for occupancy in 1950, accepted guests only in the summer during the weekends. Summer visitors paid $7 per person per day to stay at the hotel. It was common for 500 people to be turned away over a typical Fourth of July weekend. (Courtesy of John Fraser Hart.)

The building shown here is the Winburn Funeral Home. (Courtesy of Ronald J. Stephens.)

EDUCATION

In 1951, Idlewild residents and their Yates Township School District Board realized that the Old School House Addition, a barracks-type addition, was no longer adequate and that it was time for a change. It had been built by the Works Projects Administration (W.P.A.), and constructed by the Civilian Conservation Corps (C.C.C.) in the late 1930s. (From the private collection of Mr. Leonard Wyatt.)

In the face of tough odds in 1960, Idlewild, then a sparsely populated area with an average family income below $42,000 annually and a high welfare roll, voted in 1961, after an earlier attempt in 1960 that failed at the polls, for a $180,000 bond that was approved, with a $2 million dollar increase authorized for a 25-year debt retirement fund. School construction started immediately (ground was broken on March 7, 1962) and the new $217,637 completely modern Yates Township School opened on September 1, 1962. The new building served approximately 105 students in eight grades. Layout of the school included a library, gymnasium, teachers' lounge, restrooms, a bus garage, and five classrooms. (From the private collection of Mr. Leonard Wyatt.)

Shown here are children using a modern classroom and dispenser. (From the private collection of Mr. Leonard Wyatt.)

Left to right are, Archie Letman, Citizen's Committee member, Buck Brooks, retired contractor, chairman of the Building Committee, and Leonard Wyatt, President School Board. Mr. Wyatt was a good leader, a critical thinker, and modest man, who is well liked in the community. (From the private collection of Mr. Leonard Wyatt.)

MEDICAL SERVICES

Dr. Lorenzo Raymond Nelson and Mrs. Blanche Juanita Crawford were married on July 6, 1930. They along with their daughter America Elizabeth Nelson came to Idlewild in 1932. Dr. Nelson and his family came to Lake County as the camp doctor for the Civilian Conservation Corps, Camp Baldwin, Company No. 1691, and other CCC camps in Western Michigan. After serving active duty in the U.S. Army from 1940 to 1945, Dr. and Mrs. Nelson were active as providers of medical care for the community of Idlewild for many years, with Dr. Nelson being the only medical doctor in Lake County. He served as medical examiner in Lake County and chief of staff at the Reed City Hospital. Their daughter attended local school in Baldwin and went on to attend the University of Michigan Medical School. In addition to having the most active medical practice in the area, the Nelsons were engaged in real estate, housing rental, grocery stores, and restaurants for many years. They owned numerous structures and provided most rental units available from the 1940s to the 1970s. They were active with the Tabernacle AME Church and made many individual contributions to the growth and development of the community. Dr. Nelson died in Kalamazoo on June 29, 1994. He was buried with full military honors at the Fort Custer Veterans Cemetery. Mrs. Nelson was active in civic and governmental affairs throughout the community, serving on the Yates Township Planning Commission and taking the lead in getting the Island's name changed to honor Dr. Daniel Hale Williams. She also assisted in the efforts to establish the Idlewild Lake Association.

OUTDOOR RECREATION

Leisure and recreational life in Idlewild included horseback riding, swimming, bathing, boating, fishing, and hunting. Sergeant Albert Johnson owned a riding stable for over 40 years that many seasonal and year-round residents share fond memories. Throughout the summer months, the swimming and boating become major attractions. After Labor Day, however, when the seasonal residents close down their summer cottages, deep hunting in the fall becomes the selling point for the township.

In this photograph, Mrs. Cleora Wilson, Maryellen Wilson's mother, is on horseback with Othello Eugene Dewitt of Chicago, Illinois, co-owner of the K-D Riding Stable, located on Garfield in the Idlewild Terrace area. (From the private collection of Maryellen Wilson.)

Pictured is Joanne Anderson Wilson (right) and Dora Wells Ewing (far left) on one of Sergeant Johnson's horses, c. 1944. (Courtesy of Dora Ewing, formerly Dora Wells, daughter of Orion Park Wells.)

Another image of Dora Wells, from August 1939. (Courtesy of Dora Ewing.)

This photograph of Sergeant Albert Johnson was taken by Lawrence Harding in 1967. The photograph was presented at the 1969 Chicago Midwest Cultural Show and designated the prize winner during the exhibition. Sergeant Johnson was born on December 22, 1875, in Tennessee, and died at the age of 93 on August 12, 1969. Before migrating to Idlewild, Sergeant Johnson served in the 9th Calvary of the U.S. Army. Everyone remembers Sergeant Johnson's horses, the names he gave them, and how they were so well-trained. Sgt. Johnson traveled to the Philippines Island to buy the horses he brought to Idlewild. (Courtesy of Francelle Morrow.)

Francelle Morrow on one of Sergeant Johnson's horses whose name was Lady, c. 1955. (Courtesy of Francelle Morrow.)

Dottie Hamilton fishing at Indian Bridge, c. 1999, for Suckers and Red Horse Suckers. (From the private collection of Charles and Dorothy Hamilton.)

Charles Hamilton is holding a Rainbow Trout he caught at Indian Bridge, c. 1999. (From the private collection of Charles and Dorothy Hamilton.)

Charles Hamilton, Gloria Raymond, Tony Victory and other hunters tell camp jokes during the annual firearms deer season in the community. These hunters are about to go into the woods for the night hunt, c. 1994. (From the private collection of Charles and Dorothy Hamilton.)

Vaughn Hamilton posing before going out to bow hunt. (From the private collection of Vaughn Hamilton.)

DAILY LIVING IN IDLEWILD

In the woods, one could do just about anything with their home. Here is the Alexis Beauty Shop in Idlewild. (Courtesy of the Yates Township Public Library.)

Mama Helen Curry, the second female constable, along with constable Dilbert Dotson. (From the private collection of Mama Helen Curry.)

The home of Cleora Wilson Owen and Maryellen Wilson. Before purchasing the property in the early 1960s, the cottage was owned by Lelia Walker Wilson and later the Madame C.J. Walker Estate. (From the private collection of Maryellen Wilson.)

A view of Lake Idlewild from Maryellen Wilson's backyard. (From the private collection of Maryellen Wilson.)

Some Idlewild residents lived in trailer homes. (Courtesy of John Fraser Hart.)

The Sommer's Home is one of the older homes in Idlewild. (Courtesy of John Fraser Hart.)

An example front page from a 1950s newspaper in the community, *Chatter Box*. (Courtesy of the Yates Township Public Library.)

The Challenger was another 1950s newspaper in the community, which was founded by Helen Z. Thompson. (Courtesy of the Yates Township Public Library.)

Ten

ECONOMIC DECLINE AND REBIRTH

Following passage of the Civil Rights Act of 1964, the community experienced a decline. Black entertainers and other professionals began visiting other resort areas. With the end of legalized segregation, African Americans had many more options and were not relegated to black recreational outlets. This made it crucial for businesses to reinvest and improve their amenities to compete with the expanded market. However, the failure of seasonal residents to improve lodgings, and restaurants led former Idlewild vacationers and performers to choose other locales available to African Americans.

...One of the things people of that generation were beginning to get into was households. They had to choose between whether they were going to keep their properties up in Idlewild or whether they were going to keep their properties up in the city because, they were having a financial distress. So it wasn't because of civil rights movement, it was economics. When those people that had money that were still traveling and could vacation, let's face facts and be honest, black people liked being around black people. They would never have left Idlewild if Idlewild had stayed competitive. The entrepreneurs in Idlewild did not stay competitive. If you have to choose whether you're gonna spend a hundred and fifty dollars a day in Idlewild or $150 a day in New Orleans, in New Orleans you're going to be in an air-conditioned room with a waterbed, a spa and a Jacuzzi. Where are you going to be with your hundred and fifty dollars in Idlewild? If you're gonna be in a room with a mattress with rags stuffed in it, you're going to choose where you can be. In Idlewild, those places were thrown up everybody said, oh, if we go get a motel in Idlewild, you know, we're gonna make some money. So they threw these places up but they did not keep them up, they took the money they made and they carried it back to the city to invest in their homes or their apartments to carry them through the winter. Idlewild became a money making factor and not a community.

Audrey K. Bullett, former Yates Township Supervisor

Well things slowed up I would guess in the early '60s. Things started showing signs of diminishing. And, everyone has their view on why this happened but there are several things that I believe very strongly were part of the problem. One was that in the '60s your top entertainers were able to get work in areas that paid the kind of money that Idlewild just would not be able to pay. So, I think they lost some of the top entertainment through that; they were just priced out of their reach. And then the Civil Rights Movement would have changed attitudes in America that gave people that visited Idlewild more options

119

to visit other places. I think that was a factor and then I guess to be truthful about it and I believe that there probably could have been an alienation of some of the former performers of Idlewild in this world of different color. But after the 60s disturbances attitudes changed where you want to welcome people you had a need to let it be known that you are no longer welcoming. Usually people would not spend their money where they are not welcomed so that too could have been a factor in the economic climate.

John Meeks, Owner of Morton Motel
(Abandoned buildings when I stepped foot on the scene in 1992)

This photograph shows Polk's Roller Rink being bulldozed. Audrey K. Bullet recollected: "Every young person who set foot in Idlewild remembers Polk Skating Rink, which was owned and operated by William and Flora Polk. This was a place that is held dear in the memories of returning visitors and permanent residents." (Courtesy of Ronald J. Stephens.)

Pictured is what used to be Gibson's Garage on the corner of Baldwin and Forman Road. In the late 1990s, the structure was purchased and renovated by Denise Ballamy and Freddie Mitchell and became Road Runner's Variety Store. (Courtesy of Ronald J. Stephens.)

Here are two abandoned landmarks from Idlewild's heyday. To the left is the former Paradise Hotel, and to the right, the closed Wilson's grocery, *c.* 1987. (Courtesy of Ronald J. Stephens.)

The Paradise Hotel, which was also known as Heartbreak Hotel, before being torn down in 1998. (From the private collection of Iris J. Hill.)

The Flamingo Club on Williams Island, *c.* 1994. The building has been used on a few occasions since the photograph was taken by the Idlewild Festivity Club. In 1998, John Meeks, owner of Morton Motel and founder of Mid-Michigan Idlewilders, attempted to purchase the building and completely renovate it. In the final stages of the title exchange, Yates Township Supervisor Norman Burns, who wanted Meeks to help clean up the Island, had to inform him that the Department of Natural Resources required that the building had to be used for wild life preservation. This was due to a 30-year agreement made by the previous administration. (Courtesy of Ronald J. Stephens.)

MARCHING INTO THE NEW MILLENNIUM
1992–2000

As the community of Idlewild marches into the New Millennium, a growing phenomenon has occurred. For instance, Friends of Historic Idlewild—an affiliated group of the Lake County Merry Makers, Inc.—has taken on the project of preserving the historic value of Idlewild through the development of the Idlewild Historical Museum and Cultural Center at the old Yates Township Hall. The Lake County Enterprise Board under the direction of Ms. Mary L. Trucks, executive director of FiveCAP, Inc., and Deborah Smith-Olson, president of the Lake Osceola State Bank in Baldwin, has significantly helped to garner the enthusiasm needed for local and national support. Between the Enterprise Board and The Lake County Board of Commissioners, Yates Township Board, and other organizations and agencies, they have worked hard to improve the infrastructure in the community. Now with natural gas and a new sewer system, new service business opportunities present themselves daily. In fact, the year 1992 marked this period of rebirth in the area, where new business and community leaders had already been working to encourage business development in the community through the renovation of several historical landmarks. For instance, a series of business developments occurred in the early 1990s. Mr. John Meeks was responsible for renovating the Morton Motel, Larry and Judy Portis opened Larry's Nursery and Landscaping, Norman Burns established Burns Construction, Sandra Joubert renovated a historic gift shop into the Idlewild Party Store, William (Bill) and Betty McClure renovated Rosana Bar into the Red Rooster Lounge, and in 1998, Denise Bellamy and Freddie Mitchell of Chicago renovated Gibson's Garage on the corner of Baldwin and Foreman Road, and turned it into the new Road Runner's Gift Shop. These new leaders each brought badly needed services to the community. These developments unfolded as other signs of rebirth were occurring in the community. With the return of many of the young people who were born and raised in Idlewild, and the inward migration of new professionals, many new homes have been and are currently being built in the community.

The newly renovated Red Rooster Bar, which is owned by Mr. Bill McClure of Indianapolis, Indiana. (Courtesy of Ronald J. Stephens.)

The newly renovated Morton Motel, which is owned by Mr. John Meeks of Detroit, Michigan. (Courtesy of Ronald J. Stephens.)

Pictured is the newly renovated Idlewild Party Store owned by Sandra Joubert of Detroit. This building was formerly Lee Jon's Gift Shop before the renovation. The Party Store now sells beer, wine, and liquor. (Courtesy of Ronald J. Stephens.)

Front page of the Lake County Enterprise Community Summer 2000 newsletter, regarding development projects in Idlewild and Lake County, Michigan. This newsletter is published by the Lake County Enterprise Community. (Courtesy of FiveCAP, Inc.)

Ladies of Alpha Kappa Alpha Sorority, Inc. gathered at the recently refurnished home of Roy and Francelle Morrow for their first annual "Round-Up." Although the lots had been purchased in 1928, Francelle's mother, Johnella Howard, did not build on them until 1957. Pictured, from left to right, are as follows: (standing) Zoetta Davis (Saginaw, MI), Frances Carter (Saginaw, MI), Emma Jean Clark (Kansas City, MO), "Margo" Harding (Phoenix, AZ), Diane Stith (Las Vegas, NV), Francelle H. Morrow (Chicago, IL), Maryellen Anderson (Cincinnati, OH), Theonita Cox-Browning (Chicago, IL), Marian Fuqua (Idlewild, MI), and Ruth Burton (Battle Creek, MI); (seated) Maryellen Wilson (Evanston, IL), Jewel Cox (Chicago, IL), Sandra Paris (Chicago, IL), and Dorothy Smith (Cleveland, OH). (Courtesy of Francelle Morrow.)

The newly renovated Road Runner's Variety Store on the corner of Baldwin and Forman Road. Road Runner's in owned by Denise Bellamy and Freddie Mitchell. Since 2002, the original structure of the old Gibson garage was removed and rebuilt. Road Runner's Variety Store is now opened year-round in a completely new structure. (Courtesy of Denise Bellamy.)

Maryellen Wilson inside Road Runner's Variety Store. (Courtesy of Denise Bellamy.)

Kyles Acres, which is one of the older homes in Idlewild, is the summer home of Peter and Mildred Kyles of Detroit. Mrs. Mildred Kyles is current president of the Detroit Idlewilders' Club, Inc. (Courtesy of Ronald J. Stephens.)

Home of Lake County Commissioner John H. and Mrs. Ann Fant on the corner of South

These are the additions to the Detroit Idlewilders, Inc. Clubhouse. (Courtesy of Ronald J. Stephens.)

Tacoma Drive and Daisy. (Courtesy of Ronald J. Stephens.)

SELECTED BIBLIOGRAPHY

Books and Unpublished Dissertations

Chesnutt, Helen C. *Charles Waddell Chesnutt: Pioneer of the Color Line*. Chapel Hill: University of North Carolina, 1952.

Cleage, Pearl. *What Looks Like Crazy on an Ordinary Day: A Novel*. New York: Avon Books, 1997.

Galloway, Gordon. *The Bulldog: A True Story*. Morley, MI: Deerfield Publishing, 1994.

Kenan, Randall. *Walking on Water: Black American Lives at the Turn of the Twenty-First Century*. New York: Alfred A Knopf, 1999.

Reese, Della. *Angels Along the Way: My Life with Help from Above*. New York: G.P. Putnam & Sons, 1999.

Stepto, Robert B. *Blue as the Lake*. Boston: Beacon Press, 1998.

Walker, Lewis, and Wilson, Ben C. *Black Eden: The Idlewild Community*. East Lansing:Michigan State University Press, 2002.

Wen, Pehyun. "Idlewild: A Negro Village in Lake County, Michigan." Ph. D. Diss., University of Chicago, 1972.

Wilson, Benjamin C. *The Rural Black Heritage Between Chicago and Detroit, 1850-1929: A Photograph Album and Random Thoughts*. Kalamazoo, MI: New Issues Press, 1991.

Wilson, Sunnie. *Toast of the Town: The Life and Times of Sunnie Wilson*. Detroit, MI: Wayne State University Press, 1998.

Articles, Periodicals, and Pamphlets

Du Bois, W.E.B. "Hopkinsville, Chicago, and Idlewild." *The Crisis* 22, August 1921,160.

Hart, John Fraser. "A Rural Retreat for Northern Negroes." *The Geographical Review 1*, April 1960, 148-168.

Hill, Frances. "Her Middle Name Is Spunk: Meet Lela Wilson." *Negro Digest*, Nov. 1963, 66-67.

Stepto, Robert B. "From Idlewild and Other Seasons." *Callaloo* 14.1 (1991), 20-36.

Wilson, Benjamin C. "Idlewild: A Black Eden in Michigan." *Michigan History*, September/October 1981, 33-37.

_____. "The Early Development and Growth of America's Oldest Black Resort—-Idlewild, Michigan, 1912-1930." *Journal of Regional Cultures* 2:1, Spring/Summer 1982, 57-70.

Documentaries

Branch, Rollo. "A Pictorial View of Idlewild." Idlewild, Lake County, Michigan: Idlewild Resort Company, c. 1920.

Soundstage #108. "Paradise Club: Summer of '58." Chicago, IL: WTTW-TV, 1994.

Talbert, Ted. "Idlewild: A Place in the Sun." Detroit, Michigan: WDIV-TV, 1995.

ABOUT THE AUTHOR

RONALD J. STEPHENS (Ph.D., African-American Studies, Temple University) is an assistant professor of Anthropology and Coordinator of African-American and African Studies at the University of Nebraska-Lincoln. A member of the Institute for Ethnic Studies and an affiliate of the International Studies Program at UNL, Dr. Stephens lectures on African-American family communication issues, community-based research in rural and urban communities, and African-American Studies. In 1995, he served as Research Assistant to the award-winning documentary producer, Ted Talbert, who produced the 23-minute documentary, *Idlewild: A Place in the Sun*. He also has had extensive historical and ethnographic field research experience, serving as Research Associate for the Center for African-American History and Culture at Temple University in Philadelphia, Pennsylvania, from 1990-1992, and as an independent contractor with the Michigan State University Museum, conducting over 400 days of independent field research in the Idlewild, Michigan community from 1993 to 2001. While conducting this fieldwork, Dr. Stephens served as club historian for the Detroit Idlewilder's, Inc. Club from 1993–1996. He was proposal writer for the Yates Township Public Library in 1993, and delivered nearly thirty public presentations on the subject of Idlewild, Michigan, to numerous high schools, colleges, universities, historical societies, and community audiences. He maintains active memberships in the Lake County Merrymakers' Friends of Historic Idlewild, Mid-Michigan Idlewilders, and Idlewild Lot Owners' Association. In addition to his research on Idlewild, Dr. Stephens has done work on Malcolm X, Robert Franklin Williams, rap and reggae music, and other topics in African-American Studies.

Printed in the USA
CPSIA information can be obtained
at www.ICGtesting.com
LVHW011922031123
762894LV00009B/727

9 781531 612801